Learning in the Round:
Concepts and Contexts in Work-Based Learning

Patrick Smith and Chris Kemp with Teresa Moore and Roger Dalrymple

Cambridge Academic

Learning in the Round:
Concepts and Contexts in Work-Based Learning

Patrick Smith and Chris Kemp
with Teresa Moore and Roger Dalrymple

Cambridge
Academic

Learning in the Round:
Concepts and Contexts in Work-Based Learning

First edition published by Cambridge Academic, The Studio, High Green, Great Shelford, Cambridge CB22 5EG.

ISBN 978-1-903-499-75-7

Printed and bound in the United Kingdom by
4edge Ltd, 7a Eldon Way Industrial Estate, Hockley, Essex, SS5 4AD.

Foreword

This book fills a gap in the literature for the ubiquitous subject of lifelong learning. It has become a vast field covering education throughout the lifespan – from early years to retirement – and it has over the past 15 years travelled a long way since Bob Fryer's seminal proposals within *Learning for the 21st Century*.

In order to try and make sense of the journey, I find it helpful to identify four stages for lifelong learning. The first is all about compulsory education and school. The second involves further and higher education through full-time studies after leaving school. The third deals with the workplace and all of the training and upskilling needed for modern employment. And the fourth is all about informal learning, often, but not necessarily, during retirement. All but one of these is relatively well supported by educational organisations and systems. Schools, colleges and universities promote and even institutionalise full-time learning by young people in the first and second stages, and in the fourth stage informal learning is promoted by various community education networks – despite the recent and savage dismantling of many adult education departments in the university sector.

It is the third stage of work-based learning however that has so much undiscovered potential in the vast arena of employment, covering all those years from early adulthood to retirement. Policy makers and educationists have long emphasised the importance of learning in the workplace, culminating in the recommendations of Lord Sandy Leach and his advisory team in 2006 through the publication of *Global Economy: World Class Skills*. This review – accompanied by a thorough and persuasive comparative evidence base – rang the alarm bell for a crisis in an under-competitive economy that does not have enough advanced skill within its diverse workforces. The agenda was set for increased employer engagement with education and training providers. A series of government and business-led strategies followed in order to strengthen an economy based on advanced skills, but in reality the number of learners engaging in work-based learning has not matched expectations. Part-time enrolments have declined dramatically, and there are few candidates coming forward for the accreditation of prior learning.

The good news is that further education colleges predominantly have come to the rescue through their rapid embracing of Foundation Degrees, offering a local learning solution to nearby workforces as well as the much needed progression opportunity for level three students in colleges who complete apprenticeship styled programmes. Meanwhile, the low numbers of part-time students pursuing degree and postgraduate work-based learning programmes within universities is somewhat perplexing given the Quality Assurance Agency and the Higher Education Academy emphasis on employability and access. Most of the universities have systems, policies and procedures in place for multi-mode study in a variety of off-campus locations using the latest technologies. Yet when compared with the size of the on-campus full-time undergraduate population the volume of work-based learning by mature students who are in employment appears to be tiny. We need new ideas and fresh examples which point to constructive solutions rather than dwelling on problems. Patrick Smith and Chris Kemp with Teresa Moore and Roger Dalrymple have brought together experts in the field of work-based learning in order to provide insights and examples that blur all of the unhelpful boundaries between vocational and academic traditions. They offer an invaluable reminder about the spread and eclecticism of work places and their workforces, extending well beyond the usually cited private sector towards various kinds of social enterprises and voluntary organisations. They offer case studies that turn policy into action with examples including dance companies, event management firms, security businesses, and child care arrangements in local authorities.

The authors provide a refreshing commentary which supersedes all of the conventional leadership and management themes for work-based learning. They do this through developing in a systematic way the concept of Learning in the Round – an approach which brings together faculties, employers and workforces. It depends on the co-construction of the curriculum through shared planning, activity and assessment which has continual relevance to ownership by all of the stakeholders. The model involves three sets of actors – participants, specialists and facilitators – alongside the use of appropriate use of pedagogic methods with adult learners who may be returning to education after a long time away from formal studies. This is surely the key to success and expansion in work-based learning, involving workforces through the initial tasting of learning at informal and enjoyable levels, leading incrementally into accredited achievement, and culminating in more sustained engagement in full-blown education awards.

Learning in the Round draws on very interesting and familiar actor and audience metaphors, thereby allowing newcomers to the field of work-based learning to understand the objectives and the activities. This has been explored with great effect in other disciplines – perhaps one of the best examples being the application of dramaturgy to our understanding of social interaction and group behaviour in everyday life. As a result these authors are offering a very welcome theory for learning through all sorts of employment, and for "getting critical". Most significant for tertiary education, the principles of Learning in the Round provide invaluable insights into work practices that enable deep reflection through the use of experiential learning cycles – thereby making sense of all the evidence compiled by learners when they are in workplaces.

At the same time however the authors recognise that the scope of their ambition in this book is broad and that the Learning in the Round concept presents a number of challenges to recognised orthodoxy in terms of the respective roles of learner and teacher; conventional notions of curriculum; existing forms of disciplinary knowledge and the organisation and operation of educational institutions. Throughout, however, the central messages of the book are clearly set out emphasising the collaborative and social aspects of learning; the transformation of experience into knowledge and the development of a practice-based pedagogy.

The authors of these chapters therefore represent diverse teaching and research interests in work-based education spanning years of practice within a range of institutions. Buckinghamshire New University has a reputation for consistently pursuing such an agenda – alongside widening access and employability – and view their own staff as a professional work-based learning community.

Whilst it is not usual practice to single out an individual editor and author within a Preface, I emphasise that this volume is a very fitting and well-deserved tribute to Patrick Smith, who retired recently after 50 years of teaching and research in higher education, culminating in the award of Emeritus Professor.

Emeritus Professor Danny Saunders OBE
University of South Wales

About the Authors

Patrick Smith has recently retired from higher education after 50 years of teaching and research, culminating in the award of Emeritus Professor. Throughout his career he has designed and implemented distinctive and innovative professional development programmes in which a deep understanding of relevant theoretical and research findings is applied to professional practice in order to develop practical insights and solutions. In recent years his interests have centred on applying these approaches in the context of work-based learning and development.

Patrick continues to research and write on aspects of learning, teaching and development and is currently pursuing a consulting career within the private, public and third sectors.

Chris Kemp has been active in the live music industry for the last three decades where his work as a promoter and venue manager developed his commitment to supporting work-based learning.

As Professor and Pro-Vice Chancellor at Buckinghamshire New University he created the first ever undergraduate degree programmes in Music Management, Crowd Management and Protective Security. Chris is the Professor of Crowd Management and the Commercial Director of the International Centre for Crowd Management and Security Studies. He has established his own consultancy, Mind Over Matter, as a vehicle primarily concerned with promoting work-based learning and development.

Teresa Moore is Head of Department of Music and Event Management and Education Director of the International Centre for Crowd Management and Security Studies at Buckinghamshire New University and is a pioneer of work-based learning and sustainability.

Roger Dalrymple is Principal Lecturer and Programme Lead for Professional Education and Leadership Programmes at Oxford Brookes University. He has published a range of collaborative work in the field of practice teaching and learning and work-based education, based upon experience of facilitating programmes.

Maurice Gledhill runs a flexible distance learning degree for serving airline pilots. He is a lifelong learner with a particular interest in helping colleagues learn from each other in the workplace. He has a passion for facilitating learning by means of supportive environments and is an expert practitioner.

Acknowledgements

We are grateful to the hundreds of participants on a wide range of programmes and workshops whose commitment to the Learning in the Round process enabled us to develop the concept.

In addition a number of people made specific contributions in the form of interviews.

Chapter Five is based on interviews with Mick Upton, Tony Ball and Mark Hamilton, all of whom are leading experts in the event management and security field.

Chapter Six is based on interviews with Freya Holding, Alan McBlane and Mike Wynn. Freya is now working in the music industry, whilst Alan is teaching in the tertiary sector and Mike has started on a PhD.

Chapter Seven draws on the experiences of Dr Nadia Wager, Dr Ben Clayton and Dr Dorin Festeu. Chris Kemp makes up the fourth interviewee. They all have extensive interest in and commitment to the facilitation of work-based learning provision.

Gordon Vincent generously contributed Chapter Eight. Gordon is the Children's Services Workforce Strategy Manager for Buckinghamshire County Council.

Cover photograph: Pippa Gwilliam

Contents

CHAPTER FOUR
PERSPECTIVES, CHALLENGE AND SUPPORT IN WORK-BASED LEARNING

CHAPTER FIVE
THE SPECIALIST'S PERSPECTIVE

CHAPTER NINE
GETTING CRITICAL: CONVERTING EXPERIENCE INTO UNDERSTANDING

CHAPTER TEN
EMERGING TRENDS AND ISSUES

Chapter One
From work-based learning to Learning in the Round

Chris Kemp, Roger Dalrymple and Patrick Smith

Over the past 15 years, work-based learning has become an increasingly familiar part of the education landscape with foundation degree provision and other work-based programmes becoming well established in the further and higher education curriculum. This provision has become a significant currency in situations where educational institutions work closely with commercial partners in designing and implementing provision which is flexible and responsive to identified needs. Informed by principles of adult learning theory and facilitation, academics and professional practitioners involved in the design and delivery of such provision have developed a range of techniques and approaches for facilitating learning, and exploratory theoretical models have gradually emerged within which practitioners might situate and orientate their practices (Raelin, 2008; Helyer, 2010).

Yet in terms of informing the approaches of work-based learning facilitators and enhancing the experience of work-based students, the picture is incomplete. Indeed, the need for a fuller and further exploration of work-based education is two-fold. First, the extant literature and theoretical models of work-based learning have tended to speak most volubly to practitioners and students in the health and social care disciplines. Much of the work produced in these fields for informing and orientating work-based learning is rich and illuminating – Scott and Spouse's recent study in the field being a strong example (Scott and Spouse, 2013) – but the application and pertinence of some of the proposed models and approaches will necessarily be less relevant to some of the other disciplines utilising work-based learning where such contextual factors as, say,

mentorship provision or a track record of engagement with a education institution cannot be taken as 'givens' in the same manner. Work-based learning programmes are now prevalent, for example, in a number of nascent professions, such as event management, security, close protection and dance teaching where a culture aligning academic and practice learning is still in its infancy. In other more established and conventional areas, such as business management, organisation development and leadership, similar changes are occurring, albeit more slowly. However, where might those practitioners in the emerging fields referred to above turn for orientation, advice and theoretical perspectives?

Second, studies to date on work-based learning have tended to fluctuate between accounts of practice from those involved in facilitation and more theoretical approaches to curriculum development and knowledge-management in the field with limited application and validation in practice. A potential bridge between these two might well lie in more ethnographically grounded work (Atkinson & Hammersley, 2007), theorising principles of work-based learning in dialogue with on-going experiences of designing and delivering work-based learning programmes.

Accordingly, the present study attempts just such an addition to the discussion of work-based learning. Our book, intended principally for employers and facilitators involved the design and delivery of such programmes, aims to situate and orientate learning into the working environment. Our focus is on professional areas and fields of practice not habitually covered in the extant literature; for example event and crowd management, security, close protection, music management, dance teaching and health and social care, as well as those traditional areas referred to above. Our approach grounds theory in the ethnographic context of the authors' own delivery of work-based programmes over many years.

We call this approach to our subject Learning in the Round – a concept drawn from theatre's 'Theatre in the Round' where performance (or in this case praxis) is observed from all angles and where the focus of attention and action can shift across the playing (or in our case learning) space between the different actors.[1] For reasons that we set out at greater length in Chapter Three, we find this metaphor an apt and resonant one for conceptualising work-based pedagogy for four central reasons.

First, Learning in the Round captures the fluid relationships and engagements between the different actors in the work-based learning process (Participant, Specialist, and Facilitator) in both the design and delivery phases. Whereas in more traditional, 'intra-mural' pedagogies, schemes of work or individual learning units may well be prepared by

---

1   The concept is also informed by the long cultural tradition of invoking the power of convening in a circle as a means of fostering peer and collaborative learning.

one lecturer or a delimited academic team, here the work-based learning curriculum is more commonly co-created (Linehan, 2008; Ball and Manwaring, 2010) with contributions from disparate disciplines and fields of practice; academics and professional partners collaborating to produce a range of learning opportunities and learning resources which integrate both theoretical and experiential material.[2] Likewise, in the delivery or, more aptly, realisation of a session all three actors in the process are enabled to shape the content and conditions of learning. Traditional distinctions between teacher and learner are changed. In the triadic relationship involving participant, professional specialist and facilitator, it is not uncommon for the latter's role to be de-emphasised, even marginalised as the participants and industry specialists work through issues and dilemmas.[3]

Second, Learning in the Round is also, we suggest, an apposite label for the process whereby graduates of successful work-based learning programmes exhibit a marked capacity for managing their own learning and development, and applying their learning iteratively across different contexts and spheres of knowledge and practice. In an era where the notion of employability looms large in every curriculum development initiative, work-based learning programmes continue to offer a realisation of how academic and practice learning can be harmonised and applied across different knowledge domains and contexts. While the limitations of concepts of transferability have long been recognised by researchers and wariness of exaggerated claims has rightly been exposed (Barnett, 1994; Eraut, 2008; Lucas et al 2004), the same research nevertheless demonstrates that skills developed in one context can indeed be utilised, albeit in amended forms, in other contexts. The crucial element would appear to be the influences and limitations placed on notions of transferability by particular contexts of operation. By foregrounding the importance of context, relationship and interaction, Learning in the Round aims to articulate and keep prominent and ubiquitous for all parties this important consideration.

Third, Learning in the Round is a profoundly social process, (Bandura, 1971; Coffield, 1999) a further form of that situated learning that has been identified as so characteristic and so beneficial in learning and development in contemporary education and professional development (Lave and Wenger, 1991; Wenger, 1998). By bringing together the perspectives of Specialist, Facilitator and Participants, niceties and particularities of organisational culture and practice are captured and perceived in a manner that would not be possible by any one of these

---

2   Likewise what has counted as a 'classroom' in the authors' own work-based learning facilitation has ranged from conference centres, community centres, formal classrooms and lecture theatres, boardrooms and meeting rooms, portacabins, sporting and event arenas, marquees and firing ranges.

3   Not least of the concerns arising from this, beyond the respective roles and responsibilities of the actors, are matters of quality assurance .

key actors individually. This process is not without its challenges in terms of foregrounding misperceptions and assumptions which can emerge as tensions and disagreements which are inherent in the 'settling in' process.

A successful work-based pedagogy in the professional fields covered in this book at least has a fundamentally social and connectivist orientation.[4] As the examples included in this book will show, it has been our experience that learning strategies which require participants to describe significant work-related episodes and events can initiate this process. Recollections, shared 'in the round' within a peer group, gradually move from the descriptive to the analytic as participants begin to appreciate that their ways of dealing with and managing common work-based occurrences are but one way amongst a range of others. From this realisation it is a relatively short step to participants recognising preference in the form of habitual assumptions, beliefs and practices in relation to their own learning. It is then possible to begin to consider the effects of context and task on actions and to introduce useful concepts such as that of metacognition.

Finally, we set out Learning in the Round as an apt summation of that most important aspect of the successful work-based learning pedagogy – the process whereby a work-based learner no longer reflects upon workplace issues and challenges from a single aspect, or even 'in the main', but now in the round. In a fully realised work-based learning process, the learner is fully engaged in the learning process. Experience is indeed converted into learning, a process outlined powerfully in Boud, Keogh and Walker (1985) and new conceptual models are developed for processing future experiences (Mezirow, 1991). Realising this fourth dimension of Learning in the Round is perhaps the most challenging aspect of work-based learning programmes: for many practitioners, concerned with interventions and outcomes in the workplace, the notion of standing back, of suspending action so that one might reflect at length, is virtual anathema. It runs counter to the dynamics of many workplaces in which action and decision-making are so valorised in organisational culture that individuals' identities become tied up in an action orientation, to extent occasionally of confusing action with purpose.

Creating the conditions in which participants can begin to appreciate the value of reflection as a central element of learning takes time and requires patience and persistence by the facilitator, however once that particular penny has dropped it is our experience that participants' learning and predispositions to new ideas and approaches are significantly increased. It follows from this that the learning journey and trajectory of the respective

---

4 Again, it might be suggested that in the fields of health and social care, where pedagogies for work-based and practice learning are more established and better documented, the existence of a strong culture of individual mentoring and of individual or group clinical supervision already serves this need for a social contextualisation of individual learning though the use of action learning sets in service improvement initiatives. Other areas of practice suggest the perceived value of assembling a wider group of colleagues to catalyse or enhance practice learning in order to promote transformative learning.

actors involves them experiencing, adapting and re-adapting to a range of situations and recognising the potential of these experiences in relation to their own personal and professional development.

These four factors then are our premise for setting out in this book a view of Learning in the Round – a notion we suggest which is helpful for both thinking about and dealing with the distinctive challenges of work-based education.[5] The book is designed principally for facilitators of work-based programmes – but also for learners wishing to reflect further on the process of learning at work while accessing an educational experience from the workplace. Based on over twenty years' experience of facilitating work-based learning programmes for sector specific groups and also for mixed and diverse groups, the book's structure is as follows.

Chapter Two revisits the key notion of the workplace as curriculum and maps the key drivers, assumptions and contexts within which work-based learning takes place. Chapter Three articulates the concept of Learning in the Round in greater depth, elaborating how the interaction between three key sets of actors lies at the heart of the process. The means by which we have researched these actors' perspectives using an immersive ethnographic methodology is set out in Chapter Four and the rich data deriving from that research is explored in Chapters Five to Seven. The book's penultimate chapter offers some sustained examples and practical suggestions regarding curriculum development and pedagogic delivery in the field of work-based learning. The final chapter captures some emerging trends, significant dilemmas and issues along with some tentative conclusions pointing the way to future work in this important field.

We recognise that the implications of Learning in the Round are challenging when it comes to designing and delivering programmes within the more traditional and established models of educational delivery. If the full-time model of education implies a linear and consistent learning journey through the curriculum, the characteristic learning journey for a part-time work-based learner is more an iterative and varied exploration of byways (Iredale et al, 2014). Designing and supporting such excursions is resource-intensive and demanding in the short-term. However, we would argue that in the long term it is equally as expensive as more traditional forms of provision. Yet with such programmes likely to play an increasing part in education delivery, aspects of institutional process and culture will increasingly need to accommodate and adapt to this newer curriculum area. If this book goes some way to explaining and supporting this process it will have met its aim.

---

5   We are aware that the provision of work-based learning initiatives and programmes is not exclusive to any single sector of education, but occurs in a range of institutions. To this end throughout this book we refer to those organisations by means of generic terms such as 'institutions', 'academie' and 'educational' in order better to reflect the range of provision.

References

Atkinson, P. and Hammersley, M. (2007). (3rd ed). Ethnography: principles and practice. London. Routledge.

Ball, I. and Manwaring, G. (2010). Making it work: a guidebook exploring work-based learning. Gloucester. Quality Assurance Agency.

Bandura, A. (1971). Social learning theory. New York. General Learning Press.

Barnett, R. (1994). The limits of competence. Buckingham. The Society for Research into Higher Education and The Open University.

Boud, D. Keogh, R. & Walker, D. (eds) (1985). Reflection: turning experience into learning. London. Kogan Page.

Boud, D and Garrick, J (1999) (eds). Understanding Learning at Work. London. Routledge.

Boud, D. & Solomon, N. (2000). Working as the curriculum: pedagogical and identity implications. UTS Research Centre Vocational Education & Training Working Knowledge: productive learning at work. The Australian Centre for Organisational, Vocational & Adult Learning.

Coffield, F. (1999). Breaking the consensus: lifelong learning as social control. British Educational Research Journal. 25 (4). 479-499.

Coffield, F. Moseley, D. Hall, E & Ecclestone, K. (2004). Learning styles and pedagogy in post-16 learning. London. The Learning and Skills Research Centre.

Eraut, M. (2008). How professionals learn through work. University of Surrey, commissioned SCEPTRE Working Paper.

Fox, D. (1983). Personal theories of teaching. Studies in High Education. 8 (3). 151-163.

Helyer, R. (2010). The Work-Based Learning Student Handbook. London. Palgrave.

Iredale, A., Orr, K., Bailey, W. and Wormald, J. (2014), 'Confidence, risk and the journey into praxis: work-based learning and teacher development', Journal of Education for Teaching. 39 (2). (In press).

Lave, J. and Wenger, (1991). Situated Learning: Legitimate Peripheral Participation. Cambridge. Cambridge University Press.

Linehan, M. (2008). Work-based Learning: Graduating Through The Workplace. Cork: CIT Press.

Lucas, U. Cox, P. Croudace, C. & Milford, P. (2004). 'Who writes this stuff?' Students' perceptions of their skill development. Teaching in Higher Education 9 (1). 55-68.

McAlpine, l. Weston, C. Beauchamp, J. Wiseman, C. & Beauchamp, C. (1999). Building a metacognitive model of reflection. Higher Education. 37. 105-131.

Mezirow, J. (1991). Transformative Dimensions of Adult Learning. San Francisco. Jossey-Bass.

Scott, I and Spouse,J. (2013). Practice Based Learning in Healthcare: Mentorship, Facilitation and Supervision. Oxford. Wiley-Blackwell.

Wenger, E. (1998). Communities of Practice: Learning, Meaning and Identity. Cambridge. Cambridge University Press.

Chapter Two
The workplace as curriculum
Patrick Smith and Chris Kemp

The notion of the workplace as curriculum is of relatively recent origin combining two significant concepts which had previously been perceived as unrelated, but each of which can share similarities depending on their interpretation. Increasingly the workplace with its 'dynamic complexity' (Moore, 2004) is being recognised as a site of learning and curriculum – a concept whose use should no longer be confined to the academic field.

On the one hand the curriculum, as a course of study, is concerned with stimulating learning; it is formalised and pursued under the guidance of a teacher. In its traditional form it exists as a clearly explicit entity (Bloom, 1966; Hirst & Peters, 1970; Hooper, 1971; Kelly, 1977 and Taba, 1962). The priorities of the workplace, on the other hand, have tended to relegate learning to a sub-ordinate, informal and coincidental role (Marsick & Watkins, 1990; Boud & Solomon, 2000); learning being a possibly functional by-product of the activities of work, but not the principal concern, (Eraut, 2009).

Theorising about the curriculum, though not as prevalent as once it was, reveals a wide range of conceptions from the formal and utilitarian:

> *"...presented instructional content..."*
> **(Maccia, quoted in Hooper 1971: 181)**

and:

> *"...a sequence of potential experiences set up in school for the purpose of disciplining children and youth in group ways of thinking and acting"*
> **(Smith et al, quoted in Taba 1962: 9)**

to the more comprehensive and socially oriented:

> *"...total effort of the school to bring about desired outcomes in school and out-of-school situations."*
> **(Saylor & Alexander, quoted in Taba 1962: 9)**

More recently for Barnett however:

> *"A curriculum is more than its knowledge components...(it) embraces the students' engagement with the offerings put before them"*
> **(Barnett, 1994: 45)**

whilst for Stenhouse (1975: 4) the curriculum is something of an experiment – a set of intentions which serve as a starting point for pedagogic activities.

The emphasis of the first two quotations is on formalised knowledge presented, delivered and absorbed (hopefully) by learners; it is a formally defined and structured entity, whereas the conception implicit in the other quotations is broader, more socially and developmentally oriented and involves the student in a more active and constructive role. Here the notion of curriculum is less clearly defined, less directed by any one party; intentions and outcomes are both problematic and to an extent negotiated and created through interactions.

Were one to redact the above quotations, removing references to 'the student' and replacing them with references to 'the learner' or even 'the worker' then the similarities between what might be termed more complex (and perhaps more realistic) conceptions of curriculum and the role of learning in the workplace emerge.

The idea, however, that learning and working are distinct and separate activities which need to be 'bridged' continues to be a pervasive strand in thinking as noted by Ball & Mainwaring (2010). The result of these distinctions has created and sustained sharp distinctions between the educational institutions and the workplace, particularly in relation to the nature, role and functions of learning. Furthermore, qualitative judgements which elevate the learning of the academy and relegate that which might be achieved in the workplace neglect those examples of the workplace as working curriculum which naturally occur (Moore, 2004). Such distinctions are restrictive and unhelpful to practitioners faced with the task of facilitating work-based learning at the intersection of the workplace and the academy.

The notion of workplace as curriculum in which learning comes about as a result of knowledge and insights created from individual and group experiences, some of which might be promoted and facilitated by more experienced individuals, but many of which are the result of peer interactions. This is remarkably similar to those pedagogic regimes typical of experiential workshops and learning activities. Let us be clear, what we are referring to here are not formal programmes of instruction and study, but rather those less structured experiences by means of which individuals are introduced and inducted into a community of practitioners (Lave & Wenger, 1991; Wenger, 1998) and how, once inside, they acquire, create and contribute knowledge and understanding through critical reflection on experiences – experiences gained in different and often challenging situations. Such processes however are not without their tensions and challenges as we mentioned in Chapter One and as the following example illustrates.

In a Master's Degree in Strategic Leisure Management two groups of participants were formed into one cohort, half drawn from industry, the other half directly following on from their undergraduate programmes. For the first three weeks the gulf between the two groups in terms of mutual suspicion, scepticism and animosity was evident to all concerned. However things began to change, as slowly, in much the same way as set out in Tuckman's (1965) stages of group formation, changes occurred from formation to performance and each party began to accept and appreciate the contributions the others had to make. Thereafter the painful tensions and silences of the first three weeks disappeared and the full synergies of two diverse groups were integrated to the benefit of all.

The role of knowledge

The pedagogy of experiential, workshop-based learning shares many similarities with learning in the workplace. However other similarities exist. The role of experience, its accumulation and conversion into knowledge is a process which occurs in both settings. Knowledge in such circumstances is not inert, it is not so much a body of facts, concepts and related techniques to be slavishly acquired and adhered to, rather it is organic, something to be nudged and moulded, shaped to fit the needs of a specific situation. In Gibbons et al's (1994) terms it is 'Mode Two Knowledge' – it exists in the moment, it is often trans-disciplinary, heterarchical and group-based, its relevance and conclusions created through problem-solving and application. Mode Two knowledge is transitory: once applied it tends then to recede into the background in terms of relevance and conscious recall, becoming little more than the unconscious accretion of experience. As Huff (2000) notes, Mode Two knowledge does not 'linger over consequences' in its pursuit of creative transformation.

Mode One Knowledge in contradistinction is the fare on offer in the traditional classroom concerned with the search for truth via traditional, well-defined disciplines based in educational institutions and dominated by highly trained individuals and, as such, would appear more remote and unrelated to the needs of work. According to Huff (2000) it is too slow, inflexible and introspective for workplace application: however both modes of knowledge have their limitations and Huff proposes a synthesis of the two approaches which he terms Knowledge One point Five which, he claims, draws on the most desirable features of each mode.

Transformative learning

Mezirow et al's (1990) concept of transformative learning emphases the importance of taking personal experience as a starting point for learning, along with the provision of time in which to reflect upon experiences, both individually and in association with peers. One of the challenges for the facilitator of experiential workshops working with mature, experienced, work-based practitioners is that of striking of an appropriate balance between drawing on that resident expertise and experience within the group – making conscious that experience and 'locked in' knowledge which individuals possess tacitly – and feeding in theoretical concepts and perspectives as and when appropriate. In this process it may well be necessary to help participants to 'unlearn' (Akgun et al, 2007), and treat their understandings, beliefs and associated practices not as 'the only way' but as 'one way' amongst an entire range. Associated with this process of raising participants' awareness are a number of capabilities (Stephenson, 1998) which serve to influence Learning in the Round, such as the concepts of self-directed learning, learning to learn, motivation, metacognition and those five contextual factors which we outline and discuss in Chapter Three.

One of the principal disadvantages of Mode Two Knowledge is that it is too easily 'put down to experience' that it becomes tacit and therefore difficult to access, share and serve as the basis for future learning and development. One of the principal disadvantages of Mode One Knowledge is that its emphasis on abstract fact and theory leaves the individual with little to contribute, indeed too often it relegates the individual to the role of passive recipient, thereby excluding them from an essential part of the learning process.

Putting the student at the centre of the learning process has been a familiar mantra for decades and one hesitates to reassert this approach given the intrinsic challenges of facilitating education programmes in a context of rapid change. Experience demonstrates that there are inevitably disjunctions between aspiration and outcome in relation to this notion of learner centrality, but experience has demonstrated to us the benefits of establishing a pedagogic association comprising the Participant, the Facilitator and the Specialist in a collaborative learning relationship.

Although this notion of Learning in the Round is elaborated more fully in the following chapter, at this point we would like to explore the reasoning behind our approach.

Mature adults joining programmes of study based either in their workplaces or at an educational institution represent significant reservoirs of expertise and experience which, once tapped, can enhance not only their own learning, but that of all the others involved with them. However, whilst learning is potentially ubiquitous and deeply embedded in workplaces, for the most part that knowledge and consolidated experience, as a function of routinisation (Eraut, 2009), remains tacit and beyond conscious recall and therefore critical examination. Typical of this state of affairs is the issue of decision making. Participants have often employed a mixture of intuitive 'gut' feelings and accumulated experience as the basis of decision making with the result that requiring them to question this process and, possibly to shift from instinctive behaviour is particularly difficult, after all, 'We've always done it this way! And it's always worked.' Nothing, it seems, consolidates behaviours more irrevocably than habit – a position which Snook describes:

> *"Each uneventful day that passes reinforces a steadily growing false sense of confidence that everything is all right – that I, we, my group must be OK because the way we did things todays resulted in no adverse consequences."*
> **(Snook, 2010)**

Habitual and unconscious behaviours exert profound influences on behaviours, beliefs and assumptions and it is to these that we devote time and energy in order to bring them out into the light of day through reflection, discussion and critical scrutiny.

Our intentions then in focusing on the learner are as follows:

- The priority is to establish a sense of cohort identity which enables the creation of a supportive and trusting learning milieu, in which individuals feel able to share their knowledge and to expose their understandings. In short to establish the bases for learning dialogues to thrive:

  "Learning dialogues are concerned with surfacing, in the safe presence of trusting peers, those social, political and even emotional reactions that might be blocking our personal development and operating effectiveness."
  (Raelin, 2011: 17)

- We can then begin to work on examining that which is latent and tacit in order to make it available to the individual in such a way as to enable them to extend and develop their understandings. We are concerned here with enabling the participant to identify and access their tacit 'theories in action' (Schon, 1983), and those decisions and actions which are a consequence of those theories in order that they might be subjected to scrutiny.

- This process of critical scrutiny extends beyond the individual to the cohort enabling individual members to develop and extend knowledge through discussion and the critical examination of understandings, assumptions and practices. Raelin summarises this neatly by suggesting that work-based learning:

  "...is concerned with how to make learning arise from our mutual experience with others...from our work together."
  (Raelin, 2011: 17)

- Not only does such a process contribute to the knowledge basis of the particular field of practice and expertise, but an additional consequence is that it affirms the identity and uniqueness of that field, thereby adding to its overall development and professionalisation.

Of course, Learning in the Round in this way, requires, as per the theatrical analogy, a substantial element of direction, management and organisation as well as a high degree of 'cue spotting' amongst the participants in the process. Inevitably this leads to a different kind of educational interface and the actors involved have to be fully committed to a number of key indicators. For the facilitator the first is that the world of education does not have her/him at the centre, nor does it revolve around them and their subject knowledge. Secondly, they are partners in a three-way learning process where their knowledge and expertise will have to be flexibly interpreted and supplied as a function of the particular context and focus. Thirdly, each of the participants in the action has views which have validity and are thus capable of affecting the nature and the form of theoretical understandings.

A keen pedagogic judgement is required in identifying the right moment at which to seed a theoretical explanation amongst a group of participants exploring workplace scenarios – or to offer an anecdote to epitomise a particular perspective on a phenomenon. In the more loosely structured context of an experiential workshop, perhaps such learning instances are 'devised' rather than scripted, though often they are apprehended 'on the fly'. Accordingly, whilst we might strive to develop and establish a rich participant-centred pedagogy, the consequences of attempting to establish such an approach presents challenges of a significant magnitude – some of which we explore in the next section.

Reference has already been made to the need for provision to be flexible and responsive to learners' needs. Realising these conditions in practice presents programme designers and facilitators with some difficult and challenging decisions. On the one hand they have a programme of work to be completed, but on the other whilst pursuing this programme the facilitators must take account of those questions raised and difficulties encountered by the participants.

There is now a general acceptance of the notion of emergent learning outcomes (Hussey & Smith, 2003) and facilitators are increasingly aware of the extent to which they are prepared to accommodate unexpected and unintended responses and, it seems, required to develop extended 'corridors of tolerance' (McAlpine, et al. 1999 a & b) for exploring the tangential or contiguous in working with experienced adults. Facilitators of work-based learning, to be successful, need broad corridors and a high tolerance of ambiguity, uncertainty and challenge. Occasionally they need nerves of steel, and occasionally they have to be prepared to fail, and to admit it.

Assessment issues

If accommodating the varying demands of individuals and groups in relation to the pursuit of learning outcomes calls for a degree of dexterity and fleetness of foot, the situation becomes still more problematic when it comes to assessment. Assessment arrangements pose challenges of considerable complexity since they involve issues of equity and fairness, overall quality assurance, and are usually embedded within a time frame which allows for limited flexibility. For some the time constraints on the face of it would appear to represent significant problems. Participants from military, security and protection fields are likely to have their schedules changed at less than a day's notice. It has been our experience, however that these individuals are adept at adapting to change once 'on station' and by dextrous use of communications technologies are not only able to submit drafts and final pieces of work, but also to engage in long distance conversations including resource-sharing with other participants, specialists and facilitators. The flexibility presented by communications technology is both a boon and a potential burden which has to be managed.

While in this book we would not claim to have discovered that holy grail – an assessment regime that is fair, reliable, consistent and keeps all parties happy – we do espouse a number of practical principles which can helpfully inform an approach to assessment in work-based learning. Informed in part by the practical works on assessment of Sally Brown and Phil Race (highly apposite material for the work-based learning field), these principles are outlined below.

Making the most of electronic submission

Many of the participants on work-based learning programmes live at a distance from the accrediting institution, or have jobs which regularly take them abroad. Submission of work electronically by email or via the VLE is essential for these individuals. It also enables both parties to retain a record of submissions. Email and Skype play increasingly significant roles not only in relation to assessment, but to general communication and delivery on our work-based programmes. In chapter ten of this volume we discuss the use of communications technology and specifically the use of Skype within programmes and report on the authors' experience of supporting and facilitating work-based learning via this method.

Feedback which is rapid and concise is better than deferred extended feedback

On the range of programmes delivered by the authors, established practice is to provide brief feedback within five working days on drafts and short pieces of work submitted. This is something of a rod we created for our own backs, but the pay-back in terms of participants' appreciation and the on-going support it provides them with makes the struggle worthwhile. Receipt of work is acknowledged as soon as possible and participants are contacted in the rare instances where the detailed feedback is going to take longer than the five working days. In many cases the process of feedback can be conducted in a range of formats: face-to-face, by phone or electronically. The important feature is that feedback is constructive, timely and useful.

An emphasis on formative feedback

Many of the problems of assessment and of participants feeling disengaged with the assignments they are required to complete can be avoided by ensuring that formative assessment is central to the pedagogic regime – from the quiet word of encouragement or suggested direction, to the more formal 'in-class' assessment exercise. Our experience has been that the greater the emphasis on formative assessment, the fewer the problems which subsequently arise. Increasingly we have been exploring the implications of 'informalising' the assessment process by reducing and in some cases removing or relocating assessment tasks from the formal to the informal domain.

Serial and cumulative tasks

On some programmes we have developed and used a variant of the Patchwork Text approach to assignments (Dalrymple & Smith, 2008). In our case it enabled us to structure small and regular elements of assessment which the participants could complete in their own time. One of the significant benefits of this approach was that it enabled those anxious about academic writing to receive prompt and early feedback and to familiarise themselves with the process, gradually starting with largely descriptive accounts requiring some reflection and analysis before moving on to tasks requiring critical enquiry and analysis. The relative brevity of the individual patches enabled the participants to receive regular and progressive feedback, and for the facilitators to get a feel for the individual participant's capabilities and progress.

Building in reflective and retrospective review tasks

Much is made in the literature on adult and work-based learning of the role of reflection (Schon, 1983 & 1987; Mezirow et al, 1990; Clegg et al, 2002; Nixon et al, 2006 and Eraut, 2009) and we wholly concur with this emphasis. Programme design thus encourages and supports participants to reflect upon their own experiences and how these have both informed and changed their thinking and actions. Workshop exercises and discussions often centre on common and recurring incidents – not necessarily critical incidents – more often those ostensibly prosaic occurrences which constitute working life and yet which can indicate the existence of deeper, more significant issues, practices and trends.

The reflections completed by learners can be of the limited and short-term type occurring in groups or within the cohort, or they can be more formal and set within exercises and tasks completed either in class or outside. Nixon et al (2006) distinguish two forms of reflection, the descriptive and the dialogic and we recognise in our practices these two distinct forms in operation.

Participant choice

Perhaps the single most significant feature of assessment within work-based provision is the need for there to be an element of participant choice in relation to assessment tasks. We have long held to the view that, where significant pieces of work are concerned, particularly in respect of work-based projects, participants should be free to negotiate not only the focus, but also where possible, the *form* that the outcome will take. The extended academic narrative has many valuable attributes, but may be an entirely irrelevant and artificial format for participants to work within. The process of negotiation between participant, employer and academic allows instead for work-based projects to be undertaken, or outputs and artefacts of a different kind to serve as assessment vehicles, in line with realistic and realisable goals.

Moderation

The need for a moderation system which is sensitive to needs and well-briefed is essential for this type of work. Work-based programmes require particular attention to be paid to the circumstances and constraints of the participants on them. The relationship with the moderator and/or the external examiner to the programme is of particular significance here in developing a comprehensive understanding of the programme, the participants and the programme aims. Experience has demonstrated to us that the most productive relationships are those in which, equipped with a full understanding of the programme, the moderator is able to provide an independent perspective, that of a critical, but not intimate observer.

It is a conditional feature of our programmes that participants are required to undertake work-based projects and assignments, either directly associated with the business itself, or focused on a particular aspect which has a bearing on the way in which their companies and organisations operate. Whilst this can appear on the face of it to be of benefit to the company we would argue for a degree of caution to be exercised by all parties concerned. Employer's agendas might well not be sufficiently well specified for the participant to understand their intentions or indeed congruent with the participants' interests. Such situations require delicate management in order not to impair relationships and expectations.

One of the consequences of what might be termed the process of curriculum negotiation is that it extends, inevitably, not only to the selection of the assessment task, but to some degree to the means by which the outcomes of that task will be adjudicated, that is, the criteria which will be referred to as part of the assessment process. We have taken the line that this is a legitimate area for discussion. After all if the principles upon which a programme is founded refer to the maturity of those involved and acknowledge that adult learners have a need for relevant, readily applicable knowledge, along with active involvement in the learning process and a need to be the '…origin of their own learning…' (Ball & Manwaring, 2010: 27) then to preclude them from involvement in the assessment processes would appear to be contradictory.

We do not claim to proffer a comprehensive solution to the issue of negotiated assessment criteria and the authors have perhaps erred on the side of caution thus far in working from a set of generic criteria with scope for the additional and negotiated criteria. Others have taken the issue of negotiated learning and its attendant implications for assessment much further (Bradley & Oliver, 2002). We have used the Learning Contract approach in which participants set down the scope and nature of their proposed project, which then forms the basis of discussions between the participant, the employer and facilitators, and subsequently is refined. This approach has been helpful in identifying and agreeing additional and individual assessment criteria and has worked reasonably successfully.

Flexibility and responsiveness

Reference has been made throughout this chapter to the need for flexibility and responsiveness particularly in relation to time-tabling and assessment arrangements. The case for flexibility is a recurrent theme throughout the literature of work-based learning, (Boud & Solomon, 2000; Hughes, 2003; Jarvis et al, 2003; Moore, 2004; Raelin, 2011).

The world of work is often moving at a markedly different pace and direction to that of the academy (though the recent systemic changes to the sector mean the notion of the sacrosanct ivory tower of academe has never been less apposite). The cycles of each sphere may well differ dramatically placing additional demands on programme participants. Between them, the workplace and the institution impose structural and organisational constraints upon each other and the participant, who can be left feeling that they are dangling between two conflicting and contradictory sets of demands. Fitting study and /or research into already tight schedules requires participants to be adept at managing a range of agendas and priorities. Attendance at workshops can pose significant problems for participants whose schedules are often erratic, shift-focused and susceptible to last-minute changes, irregular and with punishingly long hours. Programme designers wishing to establish cohort identity and cohesion need to strike an appropriate balance between physical and virtual attendance – a situation to which the proliferation of blended learning approaches has contributed positively.

Situational demands and factors such as those outlined above vary from learner to learner. As a result some educators have moved well away from traditional academic structures and approaches towards more customised and blended forms of provision, including negotiated learning contracts which provide a common focus between learner and tutor and refer to learning outcomes, methods of and criteria for assessment means and frequency of contact.

Action learning

Different patterns of attendance mean that time spent in face-to-face contact in workshops has to be of the highest quality. As certain of the examples in this book attest, action learning approaches can prove invaluable in supporting participants, particularly between workshops and in terms of providing peer support when workloads threaten to engulf them. Our experience has been that introducing action learning sets within workshops and making the time available for them to establish themselves, is time well spent. We are at pains to follow Revans' (1981) dictum that the facilitator should work him/herself out of a job as soon as possible thereby avoiding the temptations of teacher control and further modelling the process of collaborative, peer-led learning so germane to Learning in the Round.

It is worth noting that our experience of using action learning approaches on work-based learning programmes has demonstrated that the greater the diversity of the cohort in terms of backgrounds and occupations, assuming that a genuine sense of cohort cohesion and identity is established, the greater the potential learning synergies generated. Participants from both public and private sectors who may well start by believing that there are few, if any, similarities between their two worlds often experience those similarities which do exist as something of a shock. Whilst the circumstances may differ between the superficial features of the respective cultures, similar generic issues are present, such as communication flows, change – its ubiquity, seemingly purposelessness and cyclical nature – management styles and the perennial demand to achieve more with less. The insights generated within action learning sets can serve a range of positive and useful ends, not least the benefits of a fresh, alternative and/ or original insight, the respectful challenge of assumptions and associated practices, and the reassurance that, quite often, we are all in similar boats.

It is worth noting that our experiments to date with electronic and/or distance action learning sets have not been either audacious or particularly successful. Teleconferencing appears to promise much but in practice has proved 'clunky', interrupted by poor amplification and prone to lengthy silences brought about by the absence of visual clues and the basic problems of getting everyone 'there' at the same time. However we do remain convinced of its potential once the technology improves and we become competent and fluent in its use. At the same time we remain of the opinion that once a set has formed and realised for itself an identity, then some, but not all subsequent sets, can be completed electronically.

The 'Living-Learning Workplace' – an action learning approach

'The Living-Learning Workplace' is the working term applied to a recent innovation which evolved from the Learning in the Round process. It represents many of the qualities and approaches of action learning in which Participants, Facilitators and Specialists work on location at an event, or similar live situation, and it involves them dealing with issues as they arise. In common with aspects of the Learning in the Round approach which are covered throughout the volume, this innovation possesses many of those features which demand from each of the actors a capacity for working at the edges of their comfort zones, a significant feature of action learning as McGill and Beaty emphasise:

> *"Through action learning individuals learn with and from each other by working on real problems and reflecting on their own experiences."*
> **(McGill and Beaty, 1992:17)**

This innovation represents a dramatic immersion in action for each of the respective actors. Whilst still in the process of being piloted, we have already noted a number of positive effects, for example it:

- encourages trust between the three sets of actors involved
- consolidates and affirms the team's identity
- combines the theory and practice inextricably
- enables the team to develop problem solving and communication skills as active components of the learning process
- allows the solutions to the situation to be implemented and evaluated in real time and in 'live' situations, and
- provides material for the three sets of actors to assess and learn from both the positive and negative outcomes of their actions.

This kind of innovatory practice can only take place where there is a high degree of trust between the actors and in situations in which the context, respective roles and boundaries have been agreed in principle in advance. The result is a learning environment, which whilst recognising constraints, is as close as possible to a true work-based situation with the pressures and demands for action of situations occurring in real time.

The pilot took place at Hyde Park at a Bon Jovi concert in the summer of 2013 where the participants were recently graduating students working for a company providing response teams for the event. The industry specialists on this occasion were of two types, managers responsible for briefing the response teams and supervisors who made up the response teams alongside the participants. The participants were responsible for recording episodes on video as the response team dealt with specific incidents.

Facilitators worked with the specialists and the participants to develop a narrative account related to incident protocols and possible outcomes in various situations were they to arise. The learning process involved the identification for all three actors of a series of learning points. Participants identified areas in which they were uncertain and unsure of the legality or criminality of those activities which they were witnessing. Specialists examined and discussed the participants' narratives and reconsidered the viability of those protocols which they were using, whilst facilitators observed as a participant observer, identifying and drawing attention to salient learning points and issues which appeared to remain unresolved and therefore requiring further attention.

In addition the facilitator shadowed the response teams when called out. In one case the call-out was to an incident where pickpockets had been apprehended by the police working in collaboration with the response team. This incident provided an excellent example of assessing the effectiveness of the protocols at work. Incidents such as the above amplified the knowledge and understanding of the three sets of actors, whilst contributing positively to the sense of team identity, cohesion and working effectiveness.

The 'Living/Learning workplace' approach adds a particular authenticity to the development process combining as it does the opportunity to integrate closely both theoretical and practical skills. This creates immediacy within the environment, which delivers a solution-based activity, rather than an activity which creates issues and then tries to solve them after the fact. In this way those involved in the process are developing immediacy skills in a problem-solving environment and have to think on their feet as incidents unfold. Although many of the parameters have been set within the environment, the need for flexibility and responsiveness represent

An arrest being made with undercover police officers and the response team observing the paperwork protocols.

This shows the participant having recorded the incident and the arrest on the video camera in her right hand rejoining the response team, illustrating one of the learning points emerging from interactions between the three actors.

aspects of this type of learning, which are invaluable; they constitute the situated nature of the Learning in the Round process.

Conclusion

This chapter has outlined and related a number of seemingly distinct concepts in order to demonstrate the bases of the pedagogic approach which we have evolved to promote and support work-based learning as Learning in the Round. The idea that the workplace as a site of experience and therefore potential for learning could be regarded as a curriculum is in its infancy, but proves a productive concept for realising work-based education. The consequences of this position for pedagogic practice are profound and far-ranging. They involve significant changes in how knowledge is viewed and treated, how the respective participants interpret their roles and consequently their interactions within what we have termed Learning in the Round, and they present challenges in the perennially problematic area of assessment. Our experience has confirmed the importance of varied and continuous feedback, of frequent, serial and cumulative assessment tasks, of opportunities for reflection, both individually and collectively, and in an increasing element of participant choice – not original strategies per se, but approaches which are practical and integrated. This pragmatic approach extends to the use of action learning, both as an integral element of the experiential pedagogy and, by the use of action learning sets, as a means of enabling participants to share and consolidate their learning.

The demands and challenges to each party in this approach are substantially and dramatically different to those conditions existing in the experience of full-time tertiary education, and they do not sit easily with some. Notions of role, identity and loyalty are called into question; in short, the ride is not necessarily a comfortable one, nevertheless the benefits in terms of learning and development for all those involved can be significant and rewarding. This book makes no claims in relation to any of these challenges to have developed definitive solutions or answers. Indeed to believe that such solutions and answers exist to be discovered would run entirely counter the very core beliefs of those values and assumptions that underpin the approach. However what we would claim to have developed is a stimulating, engaging and challenging set of circumstances which enable participants to recognise and extend their knowledge in ways which are both useful and fulfilling.

References

Akgun, A. Byrne, J. Lynn, G & Keskin, H. (2007). Organisational unlearning as changes in beliefs and routines in organisations. *Journal of Organisation Change Management. 20 (6). 794 – 812.*

Ball, I. & Manwaring, G. (2010). Making it work: a guidebook exploring work-based learning. Cheltenham. Quality Assurance Agency.

Barnett, R. (1994). The limits of competence. Buckingham. The Society for Research into Higher Education and The Open University.

Bloom, B. S. (1966). Towards a theory of instruction. New York. Norton & Company.

Boud, D. & Solomon, N. (2000). Working as the curriculum: pedagogical and identity implications. UTS Research Centre Vocational Education & Training Working Knowledge: productive learning at work.

Bradley, C. & Oliver, M. (2002). The evolution of pedagogic models for work-based learning within a virtual university. *Computers & Education. 38 (1 – 3). 37 – 52.*

Clegg, S. Tan, J & Saeidi, S. (2002). Reflecting or acting? Reflective practice and continuing professional development in higher education. *Reflective Practice. 3 (1). 131 – 146.*

Dalrymple, R. & Smith, P. (2008). The Patchwork text: enabling discursive writing and reflective practice on a foundation degree in work-based learning. *Innovations in Education & Teaching International. 45 (1).*

Eraut, M. (2009). How professionals learn through work. http://learningtobeprofessional ,pbworks.com/

Gibbons, M. Limoges, C. Nowotny, H. Schwartzman, S. Scott, P & Trow, M. (1994). The new production of knowledge: the dynamics of science and research in contemporary societies. London. Sage.

Hirst, P. H. & Peters, R. S. (1970). The logic of education. London Routledge & Kegan Paul.

Hooper, R. (1971). (ed). The curriculum: context, design and development. Edinburgh. Oliver & Boyd.

Huff, A. S. (2000). Changes in organisational knowledge management. *Academy of Management. 20 (2). 288 – 293.*

Hughes, P. (2003). Autonomous learning zones. European Conference for Research on Learning & Instruction. Padova, Italy.

Hussey, T. & Smith, P. (2003). The uses of learning outcomes. Teaching in Higher Education, 8 (3). 357 – 368.

Jarvis, P. Holford, J. & Griffin, C. (2003). The Theory and Practice of Learning. London. Kogan-Page.

Kelly, A. V. (1977). The curriculum: theory and practice. London. Harper & Row.

Lave, J. & Wenger, E. (1991). Situated learning. Cambridge. Cambridge University Press.

Maccia, E. In Hooper R (ed). (1971). The Curriculum: context, design & development. Edinburgh. Oliver & Boyd & The Open University.

Marsick, V. & Watkins, K. (2001). Informal and incidental learning in the workplace. London. Routledge.

McAlpine, L. & Harris, R. (1999a). Lessons learned: faculty developer and engineer working as faculty development colleagues. *International Journal of Academic Development. 4 (1). 11 – 17.*

McAlpine, l. Weston, C. Beauchamp, J. Wiseman, C & Beauchamp, C. (1999b). Building a metacognitive model of reflection. *Higher Education. 37. 105 – 131.*

McGill, I. & Beaty, L. (1992). Action learning: a practitioner's guide. London. Kogan Page.

Mezirow, J. & Associates. (1990). Fostering critical reflection in adulthood. San Francisco. Jossey-Bass.

Moore, D. (2004). Curriculum at work: an educational perspective on the workplace as a learning environment. *Journal of Workplace Learning. 16 (6). 325 – 340.*

Nixon, I. Smith, K. Stafford, R & Camm, S. (2006). Work-based learning: illuminating the higher education landscape. York. Higher Education Academy.

Raelin, J. (2011). Work-based learning: how it changes leadership. *Development and Learning in Organisations. 25 (5). 17 – 20.*

Revans, R. (1981). The nature of action learning. *OMEGA. The International Journal of Management Science. 9 (1). 9 – 24.*

Saylor, A. & Alexander, W. In Taba H (1962). Curriculum development: theory & practice. New York. Harcourt, Brace & World.

Schon, D. (1983). The reflective practitioner. New York. Temple Smith.

Snook, S. (2010). http://markgould.preposterous.com/ Accessed 23rd November 2011.

Stenhouse, L. (1975). Introduction to curriculum research and development. London. Heineman.

Taba, H. (1962). Curriculum development: theory and practice. New York. Harcourt, Brace & World Inc.

Tuckman, B. (1965). Developmental sequence in small groups. *Business Review. (April).*

Chapter Three
Learning in the Round

Chris Kemp, Roger Dalrymple and Patrick Smith

Introduction

With the increased prevalence of work-based learning in tertiary education in recent years there has been an attendant increase in the recognition and codification of work-based learning practices. The Quality Assurance Agency devotes an entire section of its quality code to work-based and placement learning (QAA, 2007) and establishes key characteristics and quality indicators for work-based programmes, the central tenets being:

- that each university must find its own way in terms of defining how it interprets work-based learning
- that mentors 'may' feature in work-based arrangements, but
- there may be good reasons why mentors might not be used, such as:
  - ◦ students may not want employers to know that they are studying, or
  - ◦ that students might be in the process of changing jobs.

What we are proposing in this book might best be seen in the light of our finding our own way in terms of defining and realising an approach to work-based learning. The distinctive nature of what we are proposing emphasises the following features:

- collaboration and the blurring of conventional pedagogic roles
- the co-creation of knowledge and understanding
- recognition of the provisionality of knowledge and solutions reached through negotiation, and
- the creation and co-production of resources.

Coincidentally, during the development of our ideas the government agenda of the homogenisation of tertiary education as a means of expanding opportunities was the spur for the emergence of foundation degree and thus the development of a more focussed delivery on work-based learning. As a consequence of this process of homogenisation the boundaries between further and higher education became blurred resulting in a state of both confusion and opportunity with further and higher education institutions collaborating in the co-delivery of programmes in one location, whilst in neighbouring locations the two sectors might well find themselves in direct competition.

Reactions to these new arrangements varied as a function of the extent to which territories and identities were felt to be under threat. Foundation degrees at the higher education level have often attracted the label of 'dumbing down' education, whilst at the further education level they have been perceived as the means of enhancing academic credibility. Further confusion and blurring of the boundaries was caused by the advent of foundation degree awarding powers to further education colleges. And still further developments have now resulted in a situation in which universities, colleges and secondary schools, including private, free and studio-based institutions are potentially competing for the same business.

As private companies begin to realise the financial potential in training and learning and enter the marketplace the pressures will increase. In such conditions an established reputation, along with a proven pedigree, will become essential in order not only to survive, but to thrive.

Work-based learning, given this context, has some way to go to establish its credentials. For too long it has been considered the poor relation of intra-mural education, being perceived as tending more towards training than education; thought to be limited in its impact; and identified as being concerned with a profit-driven extension of an institution's work into the provision of for continuing professional education, as opposed to 'higher' and 'real' tertiary education. Yet work-based learning at its best provides a vehicle through which experienced individuals can inform and enhance their extensive practical skills with relevant theoretical understandings, which can then be transferred into the workplace. Boud and Solomon's (2000) foundational work on the subject speculates on some of the possible consequences for tertiary education:

> *"We focus on work based learning, not only because it alone signifies an end to higher education as we know it, but because it epitomizes many of the challenges in contemporary academic work."*
> **(Boud & Solomon, 2000: 2)**

In Chapter One we introduced the notion of Learning in the Round as a further stage in the development of our thinking from the previous title of the triadic learning endeavour (Kemp et al, 2012), suggesting that what happens in workshops and classrooms is a synthesis of the practical and theoretical through the agencies and the actors involved, who we refer to as the participant, a specialist, and a facilitator. Together, we suggested, these three are responsible for establishing a learning context in which experience is transformed into knowledge – knowledge which is of immediate practical relevance and use in professional practice. The present volume seeks to press this metaphor of collaborative working still further as Learning in the Round. If the triadic learning endeavour implied the interaction and collaboration of three parties in each episode of learning and development, then Learning in the Round offers a more comprehensive and relational conception of how work-based learning operates, drawing upon the notion of performers operating in the round, along with those associations of adaptability, flexibility and responsiveness.

We suggest that traditional pedagogic regimes which continue as everyday practice in institutions might be adequate for cohorts of conventional undergraduates following traditional routes, though even that is arguable, but they are far from appropriate for experienced and mature adults, many of whom enter education for the first time since adolescence. Furthermore we suggest that unless coherent pedagogies of work-based learning are evolved and debated, there remains the potential for mismatches between the rhetoric of policy-makers and the realities of both workplaces and classrooms. Where work-based learning pedagogies remain unarticulated, the potential exists for the re-emergence of traditional pedagogic models characterised by the transmission of knowledge from teacher to learner. Despite the current student-centred hegemony which increasingly obtains across higher education, an extensive body of research outlining the limitations of this approach as a means of effecting education suggests that such pedagogies tend to resurface where a more developed conception of teaching has not been articulated (Prosser and Trigwell, 1999). Indeed some would claim that such approaches form a potential 'addiction' for lecturers (Clark, 2007). The corollary can only be that a work-based pedagogy delivered from this default position would consequently exert a stultifying or 'narcotic' effect on learners.

Learning in the Round

Learning in the Round refers to a process in which three sets of actors, participants, specialists and facilitators convene to share experiences, to explore practice and to promote learning. The process accepts the mutuality of learning; that each of the actors can and will learn from each other and that the combination of the three is capable of creating synergies and conditions by means of which the whole is greater than the sum of the parts.

The three sets of actors effectively become a community of practice (Lave & Wenger, 1999 & Wenger et al 2002) with each contributing to the process of learning. The Learning in the Round approach also accepts that learning is a social process (Coffield 1999 & 2002; Siebert et al, 2009) in which collaboration, the sharing of experiences and a willingness to subject understandings and beliefs to the critical scrutiny of the group is a pre-condition to learning and development. This process is facilitated by means of what Freire (1973) described as 'creative discussion.' It follows from this that there is equality between the three sets of actors in which each acknowledges and, by turn, values the contributions of the others. Inevitably over time the process sees a blurring of the three roles and the dissolving of hierarchies.

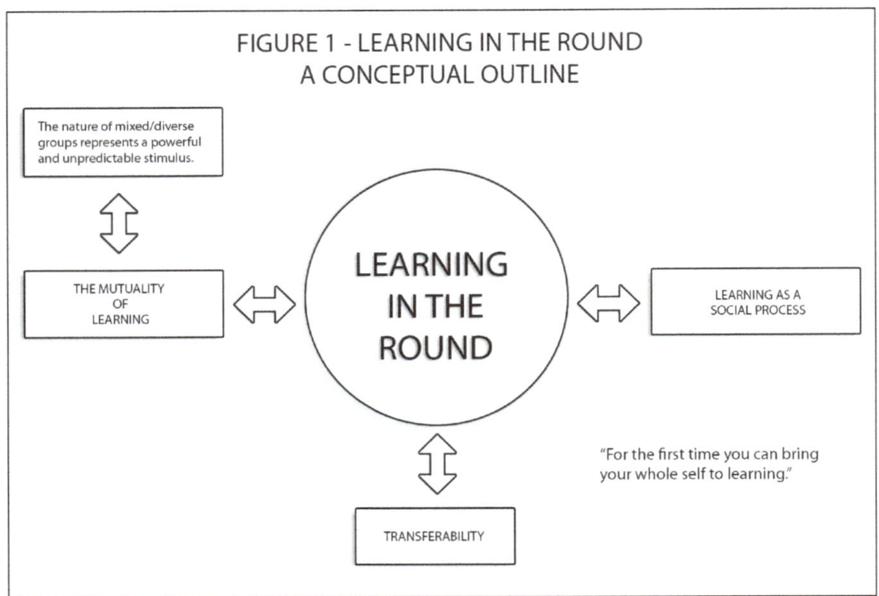

Figure One. Learning in the Round – a conceptual outline

A Work-based learning activity at Tivoli Gardens, Copenhagen. The group comprises three participants (with clipboards), two specialists and two facilitators.

Figure One above illustrates the process.

The Learning in the Round concept is simple and yet potentially powerful, even volatile, as a means of achieving personal learning and transformation. Given the interactive and social nature of the approach it is not susceptible to prescription beyond general statements of intention, hedged about with caveats of provisionality and responsiveness to emerging needs and priorities.

Learning in the Round as a method has evolved gradually over more than 20 years in a range of formal, semi-formal and informal learning settings. As we suggested in Chapter One it has been used in a wide range of settings, predominantly with adults. It is worth noting that over this period it has been used with groups drawn from single sectors, such as health authorities, golf club employees, the military, managers and teachers in the secondary and tertiary education sectors, as well as managers from large public services and private companies. At the same time it has also been used with mixed groups comprising participants from all those sectors identified above.

Our experience demonstrates that each type of programme, single-sector or mixed/diverse, presents challenges and benefits; however we suggest that the greater the cohort diversity, the greater the potential synergies to promote and support learning. This assumes the establishment of a sense of cohort or group identity which, once created, enhances the possibility for outcomes of a profound and powerful nature. Clearly Learning in the Round is not an approach which can easily operate in one-off workshops, though the interactive and dialogic aspects of its methodology can be successfully used in those settings.

Three versions of Figure Two below set out those elements which we suggest comprise Learning in the Round as we understand and practise it and represent different emphases as the respective contextual factors assume greater or lesser significance indicated by the orbiting ellipses.

In what follows we will begin by making some observations on those assumptions which underpin the model, along with observations on aspects of the pedagogic regime. We will then go on to consider the three actors who comprise the central circle; those of participant, specialist and facilitator. After that we will turn our attention to those contextual factors – the elements orbiting the central actors – each of which applies in varying degrees to each of the three participants in the learning endeavour.

Assumptions underpinning the Learning in the Round model

Learning in the Round we suggest is an organic process in which the respective elements and agencies influence, support and interact with each other in a dynamic dance, one which is at once arresting and not necessarily amenable to pre-specification beyond general statements of intention. Such statements tend to refer more to qualities such as critical reflection, analysis, appraisal, trust and the generation of approaches and solutions which can be readily applied, rather than to the specification of knowledge or skill acquired. There is a sense in which the qualities espoused reflect a **state of being** in relation to work and learning – in short to that ontological stance explored by (Barnett, 2012) in which the intentions relate to enabling individuals to develop the capability to survive in conditions of super-complexity. Thus the task of work-based learning as we interpret it is concerned with enabling participants to survive in uncertain and complex conditions, a task in which it is inevitable that participants minds are 'surprised' (Walker, 1996), or even 'disturbed' (Badley, 2002) as they are obliged to stand back from their assumptions, beliefs and understandings in order to re-examine them critically. As Gamache puts it:

> *"If learners are to develop useful, personal approaches to learning, they must work 'backward' from their current techniques to see what epistemological and ontological assumptions are informing their practices."*
> *(Gamache, 2002: 286)*

At the centre of the process sit the three sets of actors, the participants, specialists and facilitators. Later in the chapter we focus on each of the three roles. Orbiting these actors are a range of contextual factors influencing the learning process, which we represent here as ellipses.

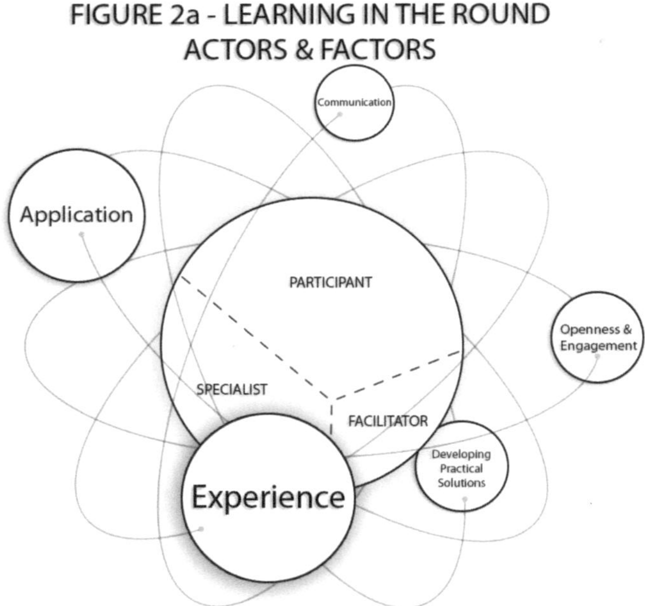

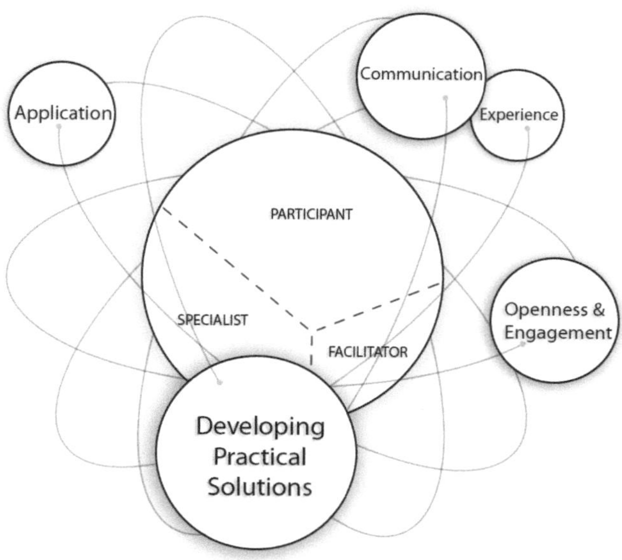

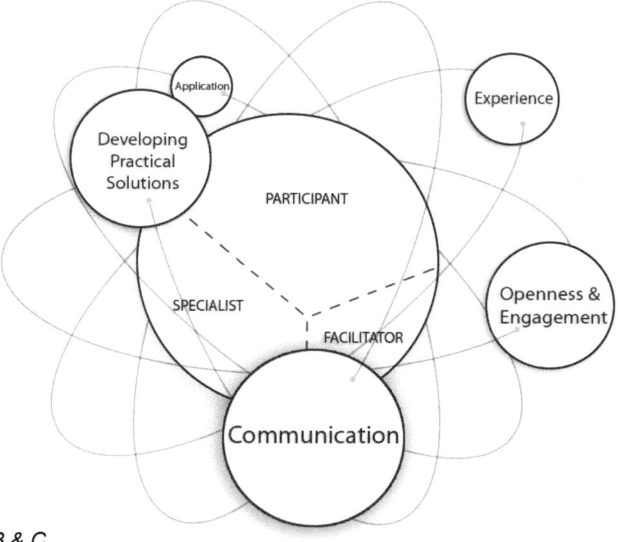

Figure Two A, B & C.
Learning in the Round – Actors and factors

The contextual factors which we identify as being particularly influential and to which we return subsequently are:

- Experience
- Engagement and openness
- A focus on developing practical understandings and solutions
- Learning which is immediate and potentially transformational, and
- Communications technology.

The figures on pages 42 and 43 attempt to indicate how these orbiting factors can both advance or recede for the respective actors.

Participants come to the process from a variety of backgrounds and have varying levels of knowledge within their specific professional areas. Fields of professional knowledge include elements such as finance, law, marketing and human resource management. The extent of an individual's knowledge base in any of these areas will vary as a function of a 'need to know' basis in their working lives. On a case by case basis in a cohort of participants there will be varying levels of sophistication in terms of their understanding, comfort and sense of identity within these fields. Alongside the business elements, the social, conceptual and philosophical understanding of their workplaces will vary from person to person depending on the degree to which either interest, or necessity requires them to consider these factors. Examples of this would be the exercise of interpersonal and social skills, which in the working life of an event steward would be focused on providing directions and responding to queries, whilst those required by a dance school teacher would be far more personalised and client–focused.

Thus each participant will have different needs. These are represented in their abilities, their motivations and their relationships with others. The capabilities of each, along with the business in which they are involved and the broader environmental factors that influence that business, will influence how they relate to the programme and to other participants. For example using the two occupations previously cited, those in a security environment will focus on the legal and guidance aspects of their industry as well as the financial concepts related to the bid process for work. However, in a dance school the teacher may be more focused on insurance and liability issues for a venue where the dancing takes place as well as knowledge of the body, its movement, susceptibility to injury and aspects of kinesiology. In addition each will have differences and preferences in how they learn, why they learn, and when they learn. As a consequence the process requires to be both flexible and responsive to all these needs and as a further consequence the outcomes can be both surprising and profound.

The pedagogic regime

Learning and role-shifting

It will be clear that the Learning in the Round process requires a good deal of role-shifting for the actors involved. Eraut (2009) discussing the role of learning in the workplace emphasises the following:

> *"...that you have (1) to understand both the general context and specific situation you are expected to deal with, (2) to decide what needs to be done by yourself and possibly also by others, and (3) to implement what you have decided, individually, or as a group, through performing a series of actions. All three of these processes contribute to your perceived competence. Even if other people are making decisions, you may still have to interpret their meaning in order to know what precisely is required."*
> ***(Eraut, 2009:1)***

Learning in the Round places learning at the centre of work-based education. However, the focus is threefold as it is a situation in which the learning is not restricted to any one role. The 'learner' in this context may be the participant, the facilitator or the specialist, with each one of them fulfilling any one of the three roles simultaneously. As Boud and Solomon note:

> *"The defining characteristic of work-based learning is that working and learning are coincident."*
> ***(Boud & Solomon, 2000: 4)***

Learning tasks are influenced by the nature of work and in turn, work is influenced by the nature of the learning that occurs. Given these conditions, we suggest that learning is concerned with working with participants, each with a range of vocationally-based knowledge and informing and expanding this existing knowledge platform with theoretical understandings. This type of learning is not about focusing on abstract conceptual knowledge, practising it to the point of proficiency and then subsequently applying it in practice. Rather it is concerned with enabling the ***joint discovery*** of theoretical concepts, already embedded within practice and subjecting those understandings and theories-in-use to collective critical scrutiny in order to develop deeper understanding and virtuosity in performance. In these conditions the ability of each of the actors to be critically aware of their understandings, interpretations and the effectiveness of their actions is crucial, in short each must exercise his/her metacognitive capabilities.

Thus each of the respective actors is able to bring their whole selves to the learning milieu. These are the conditions which typically characterise Learning in the Round, conditions in which significant insights can be generated at both personal and professional levels. The consequences not only for the lives of those involved, but also for the form and operation of businesses and organisations are profound; the consequences for the nature of knowledge are no less dramatic as disciplinary knowledge makes the transition towards the:

> *"...unruly domain of professional practice and trans-disciplinary knowledge, where increasingly work and workplaces are becoming key sites of and sources for the academic curriculum."*
> *(Boud & Solomon, 2000: 2)*

Active learning methods

Although didactic approaches have long been recognised as an impressive body of research, such methods are of limited value in terms of retention and learning, (Clarke, 2007), however it is a fact that the lecture remains the single most popular teaching method – a situation which perhaps says more about the lecturer's absence of irony, than it does about the learner. The 'Seven principles for good practice' set out by (Chickering & Gamson 1987) focus on creating conditions in which the learner is motivated. They acknowledge that effective learning is both social and collaborative, and that emphatically it is 'not a spectator sport.' Active learning techniques are employed in order to make what individuals are learning 'part of themselves', whilst feedback needs to be prompt and appropriate as well as enabling learners to have time to reflect on their achievements. We will return to the issue of feedback later on in this chapter when discussing assessment issues.

It should come as no surprise then that the Learning in the Round methodology makes extensive use of a range of active learning methods. What might previously have been labelled the lecture has been reduced in both length and prominence to presentations of no more than 20 minutes which are posted on the virtual learning environment (VLE), along with additional and related sources and information. Considerable use is made of variant of the pyramid exercise (See Chapter Nine), case studies and incidents – mundane and critical – as well as table-top exercises, simulations and 'Zonal' Exercises.[1]

From the onset of programmes we are at pains to elicit examples of practices, incidents, near misses and the like from the participants in order better to 'earth' considerations in real contexts. Indeed, one of the indicators of a committed cohort is the willingness of participants to contribute examples of resources to the workshops.[2] As a consequence of preparing and running workshops over time we have amassed an extensive range of exercises and associated resources, many of which have been refined and

---

1   A subsequent volume entitled 'Accounts of Practice' deals in detail with a range of active learning methods which we have created and developed over a number of years and with an assortment of programmes and workshops. One set of exercises were labelled 'Zonal' by participants as they challenged habitual behaviours and took those participants out of their comfort zones.

2   One of the participants on the 'Bridging the Gap' programme preparing further education tutors for implementing stewarding programmes prior to the 2012 Olympics, developed an entire resource pack which he made available to the entire cohort.

You can do it like this, without the instruments.

changed to suit different sets of circumstances. One of the unanticipated and beneficial outcomes of developing this resource collection is the surprising and gratifying responses we have experienced using what might best be termed unusual, even alien resources with groups, such as the use of the Tivoli Gardens Dot Plan Exercise[3] with local government managers from a range of local authority services.

---

3   This refers to a group-based exercise based on security and crowd management challenges presented by the unique conditions prevailing at the Tivoli Gardens in Copenhagen.

Chapter 3 Learning in the Round

Active learning methods call for a not inconsiderable investment of effort on the part of each of the actors involved in Learning in the Round, not only in terms of design and preparation, but also in monitoring exercises in progress in order to optimise the learning of the participants. We are in no doubt that such an approach requires what many might consider to be a disproportionate investment of time and effort, however despite this expenditure the effects and outcomes represent an ample reward for the up-font investment.

Chickering & Gamson's (1987) seven principles and those approaches which they require still hold good after over 25 years, as a more recent review of active learning methods, Starke (2013) evidences.

Epistemological dilemmas and considerations

This unruly domain of professional practice and the resulting effects upon the academy and its practices are extensive. In Chapter Two we noted that Boud and Solomon draw on the work of Gibbons et al (1994) who distinguish Mode One and Mode Two Knowledge. In the authors' epistemological conception, Mode One Knowledge is organised within strictly defined disciplines, determined and policed by academics, whilst Mode Two Knowledge is realised within the context of application and is often transient. Others have sought to develop this distinction, Huff (2000) proposing Knowledge 1.5 whilst Barnett (2012) suggests a Mode Three Knowledge which is primarily concerned with active knowing, which is:

> *"...a knowing-in-and-with-uncertainty...But it is still a form of knowing, a form of knowledge, albeit a knowledge which is itself a complex of personal, tacit, experiential and propositional knowledges."*
> ***(Barnett, 2012: 69)***

Boud and Solomon (2000) suggest that reconciling Mode One and Mode Two knowledge is a central challenge facing colleges requiring them to find ways of disaggregating their programmes of study in order to adapt them to the needs of different workplaces and sets of learners.

Expertise and tacit knowledge

Writing about how novice and expert lawyers differ in their approaches to reading legal cases, Lundeberg suggests that:

> *"...experts who engage in a process automatically probably do not know how they know what they know. This loss-of-awareness, labelled the 'paradox of expertise' by Johnson (1984) and 'tacit understanding' by Polanyi (1973) refers to experts' inability to verbalise a process they engage in without conscious attention."*
> ***(Lundeberg, 1987: 409)***

Not only are many experts unaware of the strategies they use, but when required to spell out what they do, they may well report strategies they

think they should be using, as opposed to those that they actually use.

In addition to the debts that we owe to Boud and Solomon, Eraut and Raelin amongst others, our thinking and practices have been informed by the Dreyfus' (1986) 'Model of Progression' in which five levels are outlined from novice to expert, parameters which were also addressed by Benner (1982).

In the first stage of the Dreyfus Model the novice operates by means of rigid adherence to taught rules with little or no exercise of judgement and in the second stage, that of the advanced beginner, the learner continues to follow rules with little awareness of the relative merits of situational factors tending to regard them all as of similar significance. In the third stage, that of the competent individual, there is evidence of the ability to cope with busy situations as well as deliberative planning and an awareness of how a particular situation or task relates to broader issues and goals. The fourth stage, that of the proficient practitioner, sees the individual developing a holistic view of situations and swiftly identifying what is significant. At this stage the individual appears to operate efficiently and speedily, recognising patterns and apparently 'chunking' information together in order to take short cuts to solutions. In the final stage, that of the expert, the individual appears to operate intuitively, without conscious reference to procedures or rules unless novel or unique challenges are presented.

The work-based learners with whom we work frequently exhibit clear indications of working at the level of the expert. To quote a colleague's evocative phrase, their tacit knowledge is not articulated but instead is 'locked up inside their heads'.[4] The challenge for the facilitators and specialists is to help participants realise their tacit understandings and actions, and to articulate them in order to develop their own learning.

We have noted previously that workplace learning does not necessarily happen in a systematic way. It is often incidental, even accidental, occurring by means of hunches, intuitive leaps and impressions. Through reflection, both individually and in groups, participants begin to recognise the nature of how things appear to be, analysing and synthesising, thus developing understandings which subsequently become the basis of a firm conceptual grasp and an ability to utilise an idea, technique or approach.

Work-based participants are characterised by their preference for experiential possibilities as opposed to traditional, theoretical delivery and in general do not conform to conventional educational formats, particularly those based on traditional 'lecture-seminar' models. Their working lives are characterised by work-based action and the realisation of understanding and knowledge through that action. The task for the facilitator is primarily

---

4   Private correspondence with Owen Grainger-Jones, Senior Lecturer in Crowd Safety Management, formerly at Buckinghamshire New University and from September 2013 at the University of Surrey..

concerned with creating the conditions which enable the participants to realise that knowledge which is locked up within them – a process which requires time for individuals – during which it is crucial that support is available from the other actors. The need then is for pedagogic conditions which are concerned, supportive and coherent.

Pedagogic conditions

The pedagogic milieu is the product of a range of factors: central to it will be the three constituent roles of participant, specialist and facilitator. Crucially, its character will determine the nature and quality of the relationships which exist between these three constituent roles. In order to be effective the regime must be conducive to the free exchange of observations and opinions, whilst allowing for challenge and the presentation of alternative views. The final element influencing the nature of the pedagogic regime will relate to the setting in which workshops and sessions are held. Experience repeatedly confirms the Maslovian truism that the physical setting is of considerable importance in influencing the perceptions and motivations of those involved. Feedback and evaluations readily refer to the quality of accommodation and refreshments – a working environment which is too hot, or too cold, and the timely availability of food and drink can be prime conditioning factors. Clearly some of these elements cannot be established instantly, but with practice they can be established reasonably quickly.

An integrated learning environment

Between the aspiration to establish the conditions which enable individuals to access and interrogate their own experience and share it with others, and to develop confidence in their own capabilities as practitioners and learners, and the outcome of achieving this happy set of circumstances, lies a deal of hard work in the form of awareness, sensitivity and a willingness to step beyond the familiar. Integrated and significant learning milieux do not spring, like Botticelli's Venus, fully formed from the surf – rather they have to be developed.

The model on page 51 has its origins in a range of learning theories, such as those of Freire (1973), Illeris (2003), Kolb (1984), Mezirow (1997) and Rogers (1983). These represent the simple heuristic which informs our thinking and actions concerning the integrated learning environments and their potential. Initially we are concerned with encouraging and enabling the participants to access and to realise the value of their knowledge and those implicit theories which determine their practices. It is by means of such strategies that participants are encouraged to maximise their involvement, as noted by one participant:

"For the first time you can bring your whole self to learning."[5]

---

5   Personal feedback communication from CM – July 1997.

Having gained access to those understandings which inform their experience, participants are then able to share these understandings with their peers, a process which allows them to begin to appreciate and accommodate differences in perceptions and rationales. Having realised their theories in action, (Accessing/Realising) participants then refine and focus their developing understandings through classroom activities such as scenarios, table-top exercises and case studies (Refining/Focusing). The final stage involves participants applying their new understandings either directly in practice in the workplace, or through the simulated medium of assignments, both of which require them to exercise metacognitive skills of assessment and adaptation (Applying/Adapting).

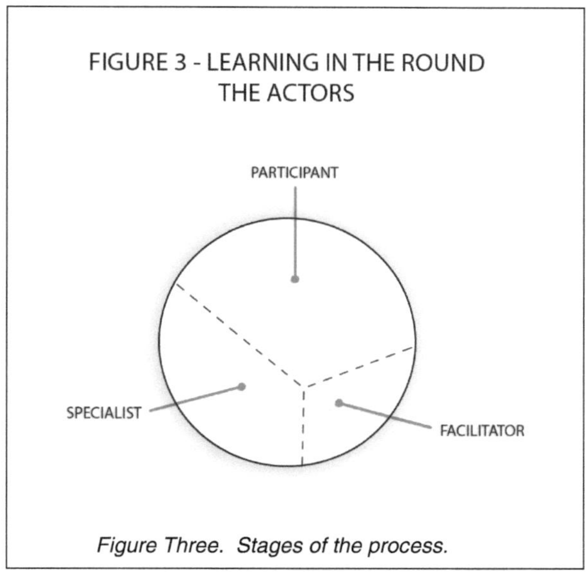

Figure Three. Stages of the process.

The Three Actors

The Participant

Participants come from a range of settings within the commercial, public or third sectors. For many their formal education ended in their mid-teens, either through the need to bring in an income, or through disillusionment with formal education as a function or lack of success and, all too often, consequent low self-esteem. This is not always the case, as some already possess an education qualification, but are dissatisfied with their current roles or organisations and wish to redirect their careers. It is still the case that some occupations remain without career progression structures or that qualifications gained within an employment sector, notably the armed forces until recently, are not recognised outside those areas. Others, meanwhile, are responding to a need to gain qualifications in order to progress their careers, or to respond to long-felt needs to learn and develop.

As Knowlesian principles of adult learning have long established, what distinguishes adult learners, as opposed to students entering tertiary education directly from school, are their experiences of life and work, which can serve as immense resources upon which to ground learning. Whilst their understanding of theory and theoretical concepts in general might be limited to the point of their denying that their practices are based on any theoretical conceptions, the process which requires them to interrogate their own understandings, exposing them to the scrutiny of others, readily demonstrates that actions and decisions are based on frameworks and assumptions and that these constitute those theories-in-action which underpin their work-based practices. In short they must reach a point where they appreciate Kurt Lewin's observation that:

Participants measuring stage fill timing and capacity at the V Festival, Chelmsford.

> *"There is nothing so practical as a good theory."*
> *(Lewin, 1951: 169)*

The Specialist

Of the three sets of actors that of the specialist is perhaps the most demanding. Given the applied and workshop-based nature of the pedagogy we are well-used to what might be termed 'team teaching' in which delivery is undertaken by two facilitators each making contributions at appropriate times. Cohorts of participants drawn from diverse fields and occupations, having achieved a sense of cohort identity and consequent commitment, represent powerfully generative almost self-propelling learning units.[6] The roles of specialist and facilitator in these circumstances can overlap with each acknowledging and drawing on the skills and knowledge of the other as appropriate, for example, individuals qualified in specific areas such as the Myers-Briggs Type Indicator, specialists in counter-terrorism, or those individuals with coaching qualifications and experience.

The situation is more straight-forward with sector-specific groups, such as public service managers, dance school directors or security personnel. In these situations the specialist is someone generally recognised as an outstanding practitioner with extensive experience in that field. In our experience the specialist takes many forms; the 'self-made' entrepreneur, the chief executive, the educational or the health professional. What tends to distinguish these individuals apart from their expertise and commitment to their own continued development, is a sense of needing to 'give something back,' to encourage and support the development of others by seeking out opportunities to contribute to work-based learning activities.[7] Whilst they may be acknowledged as opinion leaders and major players within their particular spheres, these individuals retain sufficient humility and commitment to the development of others to prevent any implication of their becoming occupational gurus.

The specialist fulfils a mediation function between the workplace and the academy by providing context to the experience of those on the programme and s/he also serves as a support resource for those from other sectors and occupations by enabling them to contextualise and translate knowledge into their own specific fields. They may often fulfil the role as the validator of workplace activities and act as both a verifier for those in the same field and as a reference or anchor point for those who work in different environments and at different levels.

The relationship between the specialist and the facilitator is crucial. They must not run parallel to each other, but ideally should feed off one another to ensure that the contextualisation of the learning is clearly realised by the participant. It is in this way that new knowledge and understanding is realised. It is an iterative, cyclical process as theory is continually being used to inform and explore how specialist knowledge and content relates to the participant's lived experience. Of equal importance is the relationship and interactions between the specialist and the participant which is often focused on emerging

---

6   The particular demands of diverse cohorts are deserving of separate treatment, which they will receive in a subsequent volume. However the principle which appears to operate is that given a cohesive and committed group then the greater the diversity of backgrounds and occupations represented within a cohort, the greater the potential learning synergies.

7   Beware the enthusiastic individual convinced of her/his unique knowledge of a field whose interests are centred more in their own 'performances' than in the learning of cohort participants. We have developed a simple means of selecting potential contributors long before they fulfil the specialist role.

trends and associated practices in the form of new knowledge which will support the cycle of learning. It is in this way that the specialist not only facilitates and teaches, but *learns* from the process.

The Facilitator

The facilitator is initially responsible for establishing the learning milieu, along with negotiating those ground rules to which everyone will adhere. The facilitator also has a central role in creating a sense of cohort commitment and identity. It is the facilitator who provides the relevant theoretical knowledge in a form and at a time when it is of most use to the participants. In this sense the facilitator 'travels' (Fox, 1983) alongside the participants, accompanying them on 'excursions' (Northedge, 2003), as they negotiate the sometimes tricky and confusing terrain of academic learning. Whilst the facilitator needs to be knowledgeable in a range of fields, it is our experience that frequently what might be termed teaching method assumes greater significance than subject content.

Working alongside the participants and specialists, the facilitator has to possess interpersonal skills of considerable sensitivity. They must know when to step back and when to intervene, when to encourage participants to 'go it alone' and when to invite the specialist to interject by contributing illustrative examples or cases. In the early stages of a programme or suite of workshops, as acknowledged above, the facilitator might well elevate methods above content in order to create the optimum conditions for learning.

Accommodating and managing the changing and uncertain fluctuations which constitute the work-based learning milieu, the facilitator must be over-prepared, drawing on material which might or might not be

Chris explains a cartoon depicting organisational culture.

useful as and when occasion demands. A necessary pre-requisite is for facilitators to possess a generous and accommodating 'corridor of tolerance' (McAlpine et al, 1999) in fielding questions and responding to those dilemmas and challenges raised by examples drawn from participants' experiences.

Possessing the skills of an experienced coach and mentor, the facilitator has to be capable of treating their specialist knowledge not as an altar before which others are required to worship, but more as a toolkit to be drawn upon and adapted in the light of identified needs. There is no room in these situations for the individual 'sage on the stage', what is required is a knowledgeable pragmatist, one who sees beyond the silos of discipline to the realisation of understanding in and through practice.

Two Case Studies

Case Study One: Managing Director of a major security and crowd management company.

This MD entered into a Foundation Degree programme with more than 30 years of experience of event and security management. He had operated at all levels; as a frontline steward at concerts and sporting events, then as a supervisor managing crews of up to a hundred or more stewards, before becoming a senior manager. Eventually he set up his own company which thrived before selling that company to a global concern and assuming a senior management position commensurate with his experience and knowledge.

Having negotiated the Foundation Degree with some ease he then enrolled on a Master's programme in leadership and management and within a short period, successfully managing his senior management role and frequent foreign travel, alongside his studies, he found a very real taste and enthusiasm for learning. He developed an interest in how companies train and develop their employees. This became the focus of a negotiated assignment for the MA programme in which he outlined a structured employee development ladder from levels One to Five. It appeared to those around this individual that insights and understandings generated in one area fed into other areas and amplified the thirst and enthusiasm for learning. Happily the MA programme was sufficiently flexible to enable him to integrate theoretical and work-based activities in such a way as to create mutual benefits and advantages. Having successfully overcome the initial cultural transition from the world of work into that of the academy and realising the nature and benefits of work-based learning, his learning curve assumed a steep trajectory.

Case Study Two: Director and owner of a dance company.

This individual struggled with the concept of work-based learning and needed a great deal of support throughout both years of a Foundation Degree programme. Success at school had eluded him, a situation which had engendered an attitude towards learning and education in general of fear and apprehension. However, as the programme proceeded it became clear that he could and would take on activities and challenges which were just outside or close to his comfort zone given the support of peers and facilitators. Being part of a learning group and encouraged to reflect upon processes and experiences that the programme required the cohort to confront, enabled him to gain in confidence and, gradually, to apply concepts and approaches gained into the operation of his dance school. This combination of confidence and knowledge began to find expression in the way in which the dance school was run.

Progress in this case was not dramatic, but incremental and it was not until well after the completion of the Foundation Degree programme that he realised and was able to articulate the progress made – developments which have contributed to tangible benefits in company turnover and the development of new ventures within the dance school field. Despite the recent unfavourable economic conditions, the company continues to expand and thrive.

Our experience demonstrates a fourfold process at work in which participants move through Induction, to Engagement, to Adoption and finally to Enactment.

Following the Induction phase the first Case Study participant experienced a steep learning curve, becoming engaged and adopting ideas with relish to begin to apply and enact those ideas and approaches. He adapted rapidly to the pedagogic regime and his role within it by relating the experiential to the theoretical and vice-versa. With these new understandings not only is the link to the workplace perceived conceptually, but also the identification of those changes to the workplace that need to be made. This process of realisation can be achieved with such alacrity by such participants that it comes as a shock both to themselves and their facilitators.

The experience for the participant in Case Study Two is different as he struggled during induction and found engagement with the programme problematic and confusing as he attempted to reconcile workplace knowledge and experience on the one hand and theoretical understandings and implications on the other. The tipping point for this participant in terms of adoption and enactment did not begin to occur until very late in the programme, indeed he maintains that the real impact of the programme struck him in the months following completion.

It is interesting to note that, whilst some participants appear to struggle with the demands of the programme and those of their own companies, the reconciliation of the two worlds often occurs as a result of the need to address a problem or issue in the workplace. It is at this point that the stimulus of a problem appears to serve as an impetus in the Enactment stage, resulting in the introduction of new practices, or the entry into new markets for the participant's business.

Clearly neither pathway is superior to the other as both approaches have their own merits, and between the two paradigm examples are other participants with varying levels of knowledge acquisition, motivation and the reconciliation of experience with theory. The implications of accommodating and supporting the needs of that range of capabilities present in any cohort represent the perennial issues, challenges and dilemmas of the classroom – how to meet appropriately, the needs of all.

Different individuals navigate the Learning in the Round process in different ways and at different rates, which we identify in the four stages from Induction, to Engagement, to Adoption and finally to Enactment. For some the Induction phase is managed with relative ease launching them on a trajectory which sees them engaging with the curriculum and their peers in short order and seeking to adopt and enact ideas and approaches throughout the programme and beyond. For others however the Induction phase represents more of a challenge, as do the processes of Engagement, Adoption and Enactment in which they are hesitant to expose and test out ideas and approaches. For these individuals, like the participant represented in Case Study Two, the 'real learning' does not begin to make sense until towards the end of the programme and then beyond it. Thus the two trajectories extend well beyond the termination of the programme as evidenced by text, email and Facebook contributions and contacts such as those illustrated in Chapter Five.

Conclusions

Whilst Learning in the Round locates the interests and needs of learning at the centre of activities, this does not preclude concern for and interest in other significant elements. The agendas and motivations of all those concerned in this approach to learning and development exert considerable influence on what occurs. As we have noted previously, in a very real sense the learner can refer to any, or all three sets of actors; participant, facilitator and/or specialist. It follows from this that in order to become effective actors in the process these individuals must be capable of seeing their own development as still being in progress and, as such, being incomplete. In exploring the notion of Learning in the Round we have referred implicitly to the important role played by the collective, thje three sets of actors, or 'The Company,' to extend the theatrical metaphor.

Establishing a sense of cohort identity which accommodates and effectively integrates the various personalities, relationships and capabilities represented within a group is an essential pre-requisite to the success of the process. Whilst every effort is made to create this notion of identity by means of differentiated activities, action learning approaches, individual, group and cohort activities, success can be manifested in surprisingly different and original ways – what counts as success in one context, with one cohort, can feel very much like failure in another. In this connection a truly integrated curriculum is essential, including serial, differentiated and timely assessments, designed to support learning progressively, frequent formal and informal feedback and evaluation opportunities, whose outputs are seen to be acted upon.

Clearly knowledge of the formation and operation of teams and groups, a genuinely interactive pedagogy, along with a broad repertoire of facilitation and coaching skills are also required. However we would not want to appear to claim that we have created the silver bullet solution. Nevertheless, by creating conditions in which the central focus is on *learning* and by acknowledging that it is likely to occur for all the actors in the process by means of role-shifting, even in the most challenging groups an ethos of tolerance and collective engagement can be achieved.

The demands made on all the actors are considerable. Each must possess, or be prepared to acquire a daunting repertoire of capabilities – personal and interpersonal – and each has to be prepared to admit ignorance, to identify and challenge assumptions, and be willing to be challenged in order to create new understandings. Yet we submit that only a high-stakes, high challenge pedagogy of this kind does full justice to the potentialities of work-based learning as a distinctive process in the wider spectrum of academic practice.

The trajectories discussed above suggest that learning does not cease at the end of a particular programme, but continues, becoming a state of mind and a way of being in the world. We made reference earlier of our intention to establish communities of practice and we take pride in the numbers of former participants who we can call on to contribute to on-going programmes as contributors and specialists, as well as acting as 'sounding boards' in designing and planning, and acting mentors to current participants. The following chapters seek to explore and illuminate that process still further by considering the notion of supported challenge before turning to the accounts of the actors themselves in Chapters Five, Six and Seven.

Rerences

Barnett, R. (2012). Learning for an unknown future. *Higher Education Research & Development. 31 (1). 65-77.*

Benner, P. (1982). From novice to expert. *American Journal of Nursing*, 82 (3), 402-407.

Boud, D. & Solomon, N. (2000). Working as the curriculum: pedagogical and identity implications. UTS Research Centre Vocational Education & Training Working Knowledge: productive learning at work. The Australian Centre for Organisational, Vocational & Adult Learning.

Boud, D. & Solomon, N. (Eds). (2001) Work Based Learning: A New Higher Education. Buckingham: SHRE and the Open University Press: Milton Keynes

Chickering, A. & Gamson, Z. (1987). Seven principles for good practice in undergraduate eduction. American Association of Higher Education Bulletin. (March).

Clark, D. (2007). Plan B: What is Plan B? Not Plan A. http://donaldclarkplanb.blogspot. com/2007/12/10-reasons-to-dump-lectures.html

Dreyfus, H.L. and Dreyfus, S.E. (1986) Mind over Machine: The Power of Human Intuition and Expertise in the Era of the Computer, Oxford, Blackwell.

Eraut. M. (2000). How Professionals Learn through Work. http:// learningtobeaprofessional.pbworks.com/How-professionals-learn-through-work

Freire, P. (1973).Education for critical consciousness. London. Sheed & Ward.

Gibbons, M., Limoges, C., Nowotny, H., Schwartzman, S., Scott, P. And Trow, M. (1994) The New Production of Knowledge: The Dynamics of Science and research in Contemporary Societies. London:Sage.

Huff, A. (2000). Changes in organisational knowledge management. *Academy of Management. 25 (2). 288-293.*

Illeris, K. (2003). Workplace learning and learning theory. *Journal of Workplace Learning. 15 (4). 167-178.*

Lewin, K. (1951) Field theory in social science; selected theoretical papers. D. Cartwright (ed.). New York: Harper & Row.

McAlpine, l. Weston, C. Beauchamp, J. Wiseman, C & Beauchamp, C. (1999). Building a metacognitive model of reflection. *Higher Education. 37. 105-131.*

Mezirow, J. (1997). Workplace learning: theory to practice. *New Directions for Adult and Continuing Education. 74 (Summer).*

Northedge, A. (2003). Enabling participation in academic discourse. *Teaching in Higher Education. 8 (2). 169-180.*

Prosser, M. and Trigwell, K. (1999) *Understanding Learning and Teaching: The Experience in Higher Education* (Buckingham: Open University and SRHE).

Rogers, C. (1983). Freedom to learn. Columbus, Ohio. Merrill & Co.

Starke, D. (2013). Professional development module on active learning. http:www. texascollaborative.org/activelearning.htm   Accessed: 02/12/12.

Walker, P. (1996). Taking students by surprise. *New Academic. Autumn.*

Chapter Four
Perspectives, challenge and support in work-based learning

Maurice Gledhill and Patrick Smith

Changing understandings of our purposes

We have seen a shift in our understanding of the purposes of education. Increasingly, we have looked to tertiary education to provide a workforce capable of meeting the needs of business and industry, and of helping the country to be competitive in the global economy. Inevitably, this shift has impacted on our notion of teaching, its purposes, and the ways in which it might be judged.

York and Knight (2006) make the point that since at least the Robbins report (1963) there has been "an acknowledgement of the importance of UK higher education to the national economy". It is also the case, however, that during recent decades we have undergone something of a change in the emphasis which we place on this. This debate was ignited in the 1970s by Callaghan's Ruskin speech which launched 'The Great Debate' (Callaghan, 1976). The Prime Minister's speech, and the debate which followed, asked fundamental questions about the purposes of education, but also asserted the rights of stakeholders to enter into this debate:

> *"There is nothing wrong with non-educationalists, even a prime minister, talking about (education) again. Everyone is allowed to put his oar in on how to overcome our economic problems, how to put the balance of payments right, how to secure more exports and so on and so on. Very important too. But I venture to say not as important in the long run as preparing future generations for life."*
> *(Callaghan, 1976)*

Callaghan went on to note the central question, again set in the context of the public interest and of multiple stakeholders; that is the question concerned something fundamental, which had hitherto been tacit. It was about the very purposes of education. By insisting that multiple stakeholders must be heard, and that educational freedom could not be used as an argument against having the debate, the conditions were all in place for a radical realignment. The relative autonomy which education had enjoyed was not to continue:

> *"I take it that no one claims exclusive rights in this field. Public interest is strong and legitimate and will be satisfied. We spend £6bn a year on education, so there will be discussion. But let it be rational. If everything is reduced to such phrases as 'educational freedom' versus state control, we shall get nowhere. I repeat that parents, teachers, learned and professional bodies, representatives of higher*

> *education and both sides of industry, together with the government, all have an important part to play in formulating and expressing the purpose of education and the standards that we need."*
> **(Callaghan, 1976)**

Barnett (1994) provides an analysis of aspects of the debate. By the second half of the 1990s, the Dearing Report noted that the universities were becoming increasingly linked with other sectors:

> *"There is growing interdependence between students, institutions, the economy, employers and the state. We believe that this bond needs to be more clearly recognised by each party, as a compact which makes clear what each contributes and what each gains."*
> **(Dearing, 1997, Introduction Section 9)**

The contributions of business, and the benefits which Dearing expected business to gain from their contributions, were conceived as:

Contribution	*Benefits*
• More investment in the training of employees	*• More highly educated people in the workforce*
• Increased contribution to infrastructure of research	*• Clearer understanding of what higher education is offering*
• More work experience opportunities for students	*• More opportunities for collaborative working with higher education*
• Greater support for employees serving on institutions' governing bodies	*• Better access to higher education resources for small to medium sized enterprises*
	• Outcomes of research

(Dearing, 1997, Introduction Table 1)

The White Paper 'The Future of Higher Education' (Cnmd 5735, 2003) went on to emphasise the ways in which business and higher education might work together, dedicating an entire chapter to the matter. The proposals included:

- enhanced structures for knowledge transfer and exchange
- stronger regional partnerships
- more embedded roles for universities in the local economy and community
- greater involvement in the skills development arena, and
- continued development of Foundation Degrees, especially work-based.

A review of the links between higher education and business was established under Richard Lambert in 2002, and reported late in 2003. The white paper (Cmnd 5735, 2003) had asked Lambert to investigate (amongst other things) universities':

"...effectiveness in supporting good research and knowledge transfer and providing relevant skills for the economy".
(Lambert, 2003 section 7.1)

Lambert found that the greatest challenge lay in the lack of interest within the business community to exploit the potential of research which universities could offer:

"Compared with other countries, British business is not research intensive, and its record of investment in R&D in recent years has been unimpressive. UK business research is concentrated in a narrow range of industrial sectors, and in a small number of large companies. All this helps to explain the productivity gap between the UK and other comparable economies."
(Lambert, 2003: 1)

Lambert had, however, noted a:

"marked culture change in the UK's universities over the past decade. Most of them are actively seeking to play a broader role in the regional and national economy."
(ibid)

Also:

"Growing numbers of science-based companies are developing across the country, often clustered around a university base. New networks are being created to bring business people and academics together, often for the first time. The UK has real strengths in the creative industries, which are also learning to cooperate with university departments of all kinds."
(ibid)

Lambert therefore paints a picture of limited systematic involvement of universities with many businesses, but shows optimism that such relationships might be developed.

This optimism is perhaps justified. The growth of the Knowledge Transfer Partnerships is positive news in this regard. So also is the formation in June 2009 of the Department for Business Innovation and Skills, bringing together and refocusing the work previously done by the Departments for Business Enterprise and Regulatory Reform (BERR), and for Innovation Universities and Skills (DIUS). There is a far stronger expectation here that universities and businesses will work more closely together, in climbing out of the recession:

"It [the creation of BIS] also puts the UK's further education system and universities closer to the heart of government thinking about building now for the upturn"
(BIS 2009)

Alongside these changes in our understanding of the purpose of education, the higher education sector has seen first a stratification, and more recently a segmentation. The system of colleges, polytechnics and universities has gradually been substantially replaced by a university sector, the distinctions are now based more on segmenting the market. Individual universities have set out their own mission statements, each claiming territory to match their vision and values.

The extent to which individual universities seek to meet the needs of work-based learners varies significantly. Nixon et al (2006) note that:

> *"...the challenge for HEIs will be to decide on the extent to which they feel it is appropriate to individually and/or collectively prioritise their support for continuous workforce development."*

Birmingham City University, for example, places this group of learners centre-stage in its mission:

> *"To transform the prospects of individuals, employers and society through excellence in practice-based education, research and knowledge exchange."*
> **(Birmingham City University, 2012)**

Brennan (2005) argues that engagement with work-based learning is essential for a university to maintain 'relevance'. This relevance is seen in terms of engagement with agendas for economic competitiveness, developing the workforce to adapt to new ways of working and to the knowledge economy, and in the changing (and elevated) skill requirements.

Nixon et al (2006) note the key drivers for the development of work-based learning. These are:

- the improvement of skills and productivity
- increasing the supply of science, technology, engineering and mathematics graduates
- creating and applying new knowledge
- maximising innovation, enterprise and creativity
- expanding further and higher education
- reducing the reliance on public funding of higher education.

The benefits of work-based learning go beyond individual career enhancements, to bring organisational benefits such as enhancing their human capital (Nixon 2008). The findings here align with the views of Lester & Costley (2010), that 'upskilling' is more than simply instrumental. Individuals are increasingly taking more personal responsibility for their careers, and consequently for their own training and development. The skills and capabilities developed might well be later used elsewhere, and will enhance the individual's portfolio.

Learning and the affective

The links between the cognitive and the affective in relation to the learning process have often been overlooked (Cooper, 2004). In their work on learning shock, Griffiths et al (2004) note the particular difficulties faced by those returning to formal learning. They suggest that learning shock is:

> *"...experiences of acute frustration, confusion and anxiety experienced by some students. These students find themselves exposed to unfamiliar learning and teaching methods, bombarded with unexpected and disorienting cues and subject to ambiguous and conflicting expectations."*

Ingleton (1995), in a powerful piece, notes the significant impact which shame, pride, power and competitiveness can have on women. This was evidenced not only in their early years of learning, but also continuing throughout life. She went on to suggest, however, that:

> *"Acknowledgement of students as people with emotions such as hope and fear, pride and shame, will engage them more confidently in learning..."*
> **(Ingleton, 1995)**

The problems which students from some backgrounds face in gaining employment in the first place (some ethnic groups; those from poorer socioeconomic backgrounds) (Pegg et al 2012) align also with the findings of Farwell et al (2008). She reported differential academic attainment depending on ethnic groupings, and on-going gender imbalances. The problems which underpin these differences will clearly increase the sense of learning shock for many. For most work-based learners, this is exacerbated by the feeling that they are outsiders, and that the university campus is for the 'young' (Costley et al 2011).

Feelings of vulnerability can so readily reduce the potential for learning. Work-based learning necessarily involves a form of exposure to risk which can be debilitating, and which can encourage a withdrawal into an approach to the process which is safe but lacking in benefit.

Sappington (1984) notes the importance of the learning environment being 'emotionally safe'. Only then, he argues, will learners feel able to take the kinds of risk which can lead to real change.

Entwistle (2001) suggests that a fear of failure produces behaviours associated with surface approaches to learning. For deep learning to take place, he suggests, the motivation of the learner must be intrinsic. If this is to happen, there is a need to develop coping strategies for the natural stresses of the process, alongside an appreciation of the benefits which it can bring.

Scherer & Tran (2001: 373) consider the impact of the emotions in each 'phase' in the learning process: readiness to learn, working with new information, conferring significance, memorising, transfer and generalising, and disposition to reproduce. They argue that in respect of each of these phases, the emotions play a part in the approach taken, both in terms of individual learning, and in organisational learning. Differences in disposition between individuals will, they suggest, determine those approaches which might be acceptable to people. In peer discussion, individuals sometimes need to cope with evidence that their understanding of their own competences in particular teaching settings might not be entirely accurate. This can cause 'consternation, surprise and often irritation' (ibid: 376). This, they argue in terms of any kind of new learning, where that new information is incompatible with an existing schema. How much more might this be the case when individual competence is to be reconsidered?

Kolb & Kolb (2006) also note the significance of the affective. Again, they suggest negative emotions can block learning, and so the key question will relate to how we might deal with the anxieties whilst extending our sense of value in the process itself:

> *"...it appears that feelings and emotions have primacy in determining whether and what we learn. Negative emotions such as fear and anxiety can block learning, while positive feelings of attraction and interest may be essential for learning."*
> *(Kolb & Kolb, 2006: 57)*

In a quantitative study of undergraduates learning basic computer theory, Craig et al (2004) investigated relationships between observed changes in learning and six affective 'states'. These were boredom, confusion, eureka, flow (the opposite to boredom), frustration and 'neutral'. Whilst boredom was a significant contra-indicator to learning, both flow and confusion led to enhanced learning. Indeed, the study found that:

> *"The positive correlation between confusion and learning is consistent with a model that assumes that cognitive disequilibrium is one precursor to deep learning."*
> *(Craig et al, 2004: 241)*

This cognitive disequilibrium might have been at first disturbing, but its effects were positive. In the light of the foregoing studies, however, it seems advisable to try to ensure that this sense of initial confusion is not associated also with a sense of unacceptably high exposure to risk. Preventing this sense of exposure, whilst maintaining the challenge of confusion, is at the heart of this applied learning context for lecturers. Akgun (2003) concurs with this position, suggesting that:

> *"Emotions such as fear, excitement, anxiety, and so on, drive, inhibit, and guide the learning process."*
> *(Akgun, 2003: 852)*

Dirkx et al (2006) deal with the affective in relation to students working on international educational exchange programmes. The sense of being an outsider is real and can be destabilising:

> *"Recognising, describing, and elaborating the specific contexts in which emotions arise are critical to developing greater awareness of one's self. Emotions are often associated with specific images... that help connect evocative stimuli within the present social context with prior, unconscious emotion-laden experiences. They facilitate understanding of the deep personal engagement reflected in powerful emotions."*
> *(Dirkx et al, 2006: 5)*

For Griffiths et al (2004), this sense of being an outsider adds to the learning shock. Whereas this can be seen in 'cultural differences' in a generic sense, it can also relate to differences in approach and expectation which form the academic and professional cultures.

The notion that risk and threat are tightly bound up with adult learning is well established amongst adult learning practitioners. Cross (1981: 133) noted that where confidence of success is low, then educators need to "create more educational opportunities with low levels of risk and threat."

The risks which professionals take in their inter-relationships can be quite significant. There is potential for 'workplace devaluation' (Klunk, 1999). In her deep interviews with professionals who had suffered significant deterioration in their relationships at work as a result of incidents or attitudes, Klunk explores the ways in which these people had dealt with their situations. She notes that:

> *"Emotions play a vital role in the experience of professionals' workplace devaluation, especially the first physiological response when the awareness of devaluation emerges and is perceived as a threat. The influences of the emotions continue as a primary motivator for the professional to continue to work through the issues or become stuck in avoidance or denial of the experience.*
> ***(Klunk, 1999: 21)***

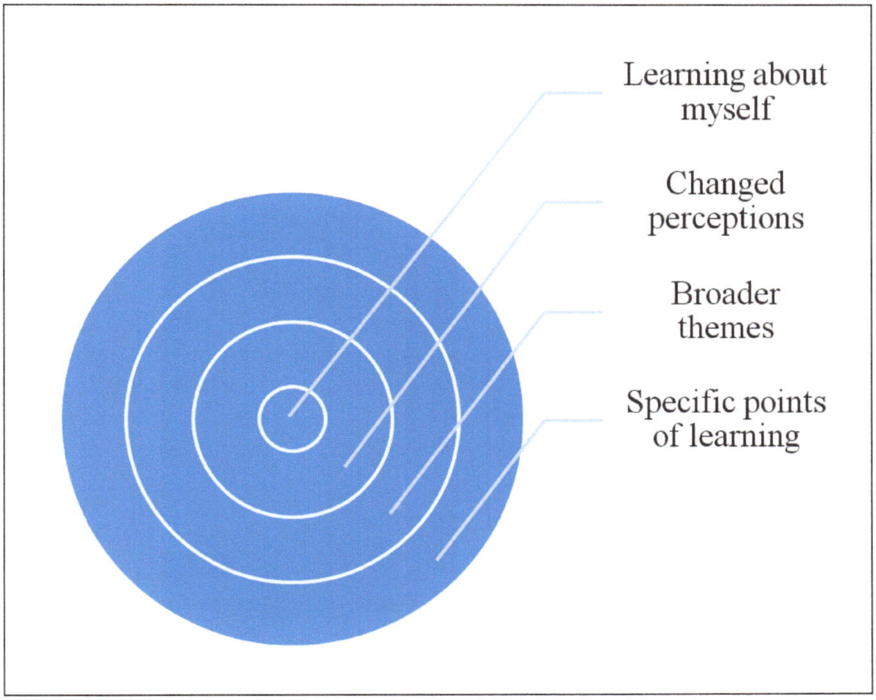

Figure One: Model of participant gains from the observation process

In a study of work-based learners developing their teaching skills in higher education through the peer observation of teaching (Gledhill 2010), participants were very aware of the dangers to which they might become exposed. This was particularly the case in situations where the peer partner was imposed, not known to them already, or perhaps known, but held in some suspicion.

The gains from the process are best considered in terms of their impact on the participant. In the figure on page 67, the outer circle represents learning about very specific techniques and tools, such as the use of PowerPoint in teaching, or an application of handouts. The next layer represents deeper gains, such as the adoption of alternative teaching styles. The next layer concerns changes to perceptions of aspects of teaching, such as approaches to the student/ lecturer relationship. The inner layer concerns changes in an individual participant's perception of themselves in relation to peers and their role as a teacher.

Supported challenge

Whilst many work-based learners are maturer in years than those we could once call 'traditional' students, these two groups of learners share many attributes in common. Indeed, the approaches to learning which students exhibit are largely a consequence of their being human. The student condition is simply a particular case of the human condition – chat with tutors or students on programmes of lecturer development and the story is always the same. When university lecturers embark on these programmes, they rapidly develop many of the habits of their own students – habits which in many cases they have bemoaned. This, of course, then brings back memories of their own undergraduate studies, and their own bad habits which have returned once more!

The daily lives of students are unrecognisably different from that which was the common experience a generation ago. Too often, however, we offer students a fare which has changed little in these past decades. In particular, whereas we have developed programmes which are more applied and business related, our methods and approaches are no longer fit for purpose. Over a period of maybe ten or 20 years, and increasingly more recently, we have sold students short.

Take a snapshot of the students in a university today. Here are just three you'll meet.

> **Kaz** right now is a vibrant, intellectually buzzing individual, full of ideas and embracing the transformational impact of his learning on his life. He applies the models and concepts about which he is learning, in the working environments with which he is associated. He appreciates the significance of his learning for his development

as an individual, and he feels the benefits of his learning throughout all aspects of his life. He needs to be encouraged to keep on keeping on – to carry on reaching forward.

Sam has many pressures. These are drawing her to focus less on her learning than she would like. For example, the demands of long hours in paid work, volunteering, family and social life conspire to reduce her time commitment to serious, sustained study. Sam needs to be encouraged to set the demands of her study alongside these other demands in her life. She needs *balancing forces*, without which it really is difficult for her to prioritise her study, when faced with so many other demands on her time and energies.

Billy simply does not wish to be part of this community of learning at all. He sees his study as a low priority, and engages in a limited and superficial manner with the University. He does not value the academic pursuits. He sees his enrolment on his programme of study as a necessary evil in a competitive working world, in which those with qualifications have an edge. Billy needs to be encouraged, perhaps in a quite robust and sustained way, to re-orientate his focus and to join (or re-join) the community of learning.

Now these are not fixed approaches. This is a snapshot. Our task is to encourage all students to develop a balanced, serious approach to their studies, in which they will be in control, guided by the expectations which the University sets out.

The notion of 'supported challenge' is simply a statement of the working relationship between students and the University which might encourage students to move forward with this balanced, serious approach to their studies. As with the development of people in any context, we need the twin components of challenge and support to make this possible. It's how we move on in any area of our lives. It's how we move on as learners.

The sector has seen massive change. Perhaps we were unprepared for that change, or at least thrown by it. In trying to respond, we have lost sight of the central role of universities in the lives of students. There are all sorts of very understandable reasons why we have lost sight of our central mission. Nontheless it is broadly fair to say we have made a number of fundamental errors across the sector, some of them more marked in some institutions than in others.

The Higher Education Policy Institute has published surveys of the academic experience of students in English universities since 2006. (Bekhradnia, 2009). These studies deal with some sensitive issues, including differential 'demand' of courses from institution to institution, and subject to subject. Whilst the instruments rely to some degree on students being able to recall their time spent on their studies, and for students to be open, the differences between departments seem to suggest the need to investigate this further. (Bekhradnia 2009: 3-9). A European comparison has given further weight to these concerns. The report also commends institutions for the developing clarity about their offer and what students might expect from them, but suggests there is a need to be more explicit about 'the circumstances in which different levels of contact are acceptable...' (Bekhradnia, 2009: 11).

Central to our difficulties are these issues:

- The student of today lives within a context which is radically different from that of 35 years go. We have failed to acknowledge these changes in the way in which we try to help students along their learning journeys. We have allowed a gap to grow, between the needs of students and our provision.

- We have made the same, shameful assumptions about some of our students as were made in 'sink' schools on 'sink' estates in the sixties and seventies. In doing so, we have created self-fulfilling prophesies, about what 'our kind of students' can and cannot achieve.

- We have misunderstood the implications of the stratification, and more recently the segmentation, of the university sector. We have failed to emphasise that the central purpose of student engagement with universities is to study, to learn, to change. We know that students will begin with us at different stages of maturity in this process. Nonetheless, we have no alternative or differentiated arrangements to offer students.

- We have developed assessment in a way which is too independent of the student learning journey. In doing so, we have inadvertently encouraged some students to focus on the processes of assessment rather than on their learning journeys.

- In considering student satisfaction, we have concentrated too much on hygiene factors, the improvement in which can never do more than make students marginally less unhappy. Whilst not neglecting these things, we must appreciate that strong student learning will result in their radical transformation, bringing benefits to student lives including enhanced morale, greater motivation, stronger self confidence, a sense of purpose and self esteem.

In addressing the mismatches between the offer and the need, we have set out the notion of 'supported challenge'. The definition and outline of what this entails is given here. Now there can be little in this notion which would be contentious. Why is this not the understanding which all stakeholders would already embrace?

With the advent of instruments like the National Student Survey, universities have been re-focusing their attention so directly on what gets measured that they have lost their focus on their role in helping students to study, and learn, and change. 'Supported challenge' is simply an attempt to encourage all stakeholders to keep the focus sharp and clear. Only with that focus will we be able to help students along their learning journeys, and empower them to gain the maximum benefit from their studies.

Features of supported challenge

Supported challenge is an environment in which students and employees of the university community appreciate that learning is the key purpose in student involvement with the university. Students work seriously to develop their knowledge, understanding and application of the discipline/ area of study and are self-aware and reflective in this process. They become increasingly conscious of the approaches which they are adopting in their learning, acknowledging that their approaches are not fixed, but can be shaped according to context and stages of development and, as a consequence, metacognitive skills are developed.

Each student takes personal responsibility for her/his own learning, in an active relationship with employees and fellow students. They develop an increasing appreciation of their achievements, areas for further development and the provision available to help them to move forward. They assume responsibility for setting personal goals with the help of tutors and others, mindful always of their central mission - to study, to learn, to change. As active members of the communities of learning, they make full use of the available resources. Individually and collectively, they see it as part of their responsibility to ensure that the university is aware of those areas where they perceive gaps in the provision.

University employees work across boundaries to challenge and support students in their learning journey - challenge to encourage progress, support to enable it. This involves inducting students into the supported challenge environment. It means modelling good practice, sharing their own passion for learning with the other actors involved. It requires offering support by using the most appropriate resources and setting out assessments which challenge students, encouraging them to take the learning journey, and judging the progress which each of them is making. It means ensuring that feedback is fully integrated into the whole curriculum by using informal and formal means to ensure that students are aware of judgements on their learning journey, and advising on how this might be progressed. Finally it involves stepping in and challenging groups or individuals, opening a discussion of areas where it is felt that the students need to reconsider their engagement, focus or achievement. It is important to make these challenges for students at all stages of their development, without giving up on any, while, at the same time, continuing to make them aware of the support networks.

Students see the learning process as one which will change them and they embrace this with enthusiasm, acknowledging that it brings risks which they must work through with help from the university and from others. They appreciate that the process will cost them a good deal of time and effort, and that this will require them to make decisions about their priorities. Inevitably they come to the realisation that the process has the capability of significantly enhancing their lives.

Conclusion

Mature adults entering higher education bring with them the same baggage of expectation, apprehension and scepticism as their conventional undergraduate peers. However in addition they also bring with them considerable resources in terms of experience and expertise, both of which are often buried, and tacit. For them the need for supported challenge is particularly acute and the ways in which that supported challenge are realised in practice require facilitators and others associated with the learning process such as sector specialists, to be informed and sensitive to the participants' needs.

In the next three chapters we will be exploring how the respective actors in the Learning in the Round process understand and interpret their roles and what they have learned from the process.

References

Akgun, E.A., Lynn, G.S. & Byrne, J.C. (2003). Organisational Learning: a socio-cognitive framework. *Human Relations* 55 (7). London, Sage.

Barnett, R. (1994). The limits of competence. Buckingham, SRHE/OU Press.

Bekhradnia, B (2009). The Academic Experience of Students in English Universities: 2009 Report. Oxford. Higher Education Policy Institute.

Birmingham City University (2012). Mission statement. Available at: http://www.bcu. ac.uk/about-us/corporate-information/missions-statement. Accessed 28:08:12

BIS (2009). *New Department for Business, Innovation and Skills.* Announcement press release. Available at http://www.berr.gov.uk/aboutus/pressroom/page51711.html Accessed 01:09:12

Brennan L (2005). Integrating work-based learning into higher education: a guide to good practice. Bolton. University Vocational Awards Council.

Callaghan J. (1976). Towards a national Debate. Speech by The Prime Minister James Callaghan at Ruskin College, Oxford 18 October 1976. Available at: http://education. guardian.co.uk/thegreatdebate/story/0,9860,574645,00.html Accessed 01:09:12

Cooper, B. (2004). Empathy, interaction and caring: teachers' roles in a constrained environment. *Pastoral care in education 22 (3),12-21.*

Costley C, Shukla N, Inceoglu I (2011). Work-based learners' engagement with the university. an exploratory study. York. Higher Education Academy

Craig, S.D., Graesser, A.C., Sullins, J. & Gholson, B (2004). Affect and learning: an exploratory look into the role of affect in learning with AutoTutor. *Journal of Educational Media. 29 (3) 241-250*

Cross, K.P. (1981). Adults as learners: Increasing participation and facilitating learning. San Francisco, CA. Jossey-Bass.

Dearing, R (1997). Report of the National Committee of Inquiry into Higher Education (The Dearing Report) Available at: http://www.leeds.ac.uk/educol/ncihe/ (accessed 24:04:09).

Dirkx, J. et al (2006). Beyond Culture Shock: The Meaning of Affect and Emotions in International Educational Experience. Paper Presented at the Midwest Research-to Practice Conference in Adult, Continuing, and Community Education, University of Missouri-St. Louis, St. Louis, MO, October 4-6.

Entwistle, N. (2001). Styles of learning and approaches to studying in higher education Kybernetes 30 (5/6) Available at:

http://www.emeraldinsight.com/Insight/ViewContentServlet;jsessionid=F63BCB3 49B86799F4526FA1E7AD575DD?Filename=Published/EmeraldFullTextArticle/ Pdf/0670300508.pdf (Accessed 01:09:12)

Farwell, R. (2008). Ethnicity, gender and degree attainment project. Final Report. York. Higher Education Academy.

Gibbs, G. & Coffey, M. (2004). The impact of training of university teachers on their teaching skills, their approach to teaching and the approach to learning of their students. *Active learning in higher education 5 (1) 87-100.*

Gledhill M (2010). Supporting and developing teachers in higher education using the observation of teaching. Doctoral thesis. Leeds. Leeds Metropolitan University

Griffiths, D.S, Winstanley, D., Gabriel, Y. (2004). Learning Shock- the trauma of return to formal learning. Tanaka Business School Discussion Papers TBS/DP04/31. London. Tanaka Business School.

Hussey, T. & Smith, P. (2003). The Uses of Learning outcomes. *Teaching in Higher Education* 8 (3), *357-368.*

Ingleton, C (1995). Gender and learning: Does emotion make a difference? *Higher Education* 30 *323-335*

Klunk, C.D. (1999).Workplace devaluation: *Learning form experience.* Ph.D. thesis, Virginia State University.

Kolb, A.Y. & Kolb, D.A. (2006). Learning Styles and Learning Spaces: A Review of the Multidisciplinary Application of Experiential Learning Theory in *Higher Education Working Paper 5/05*, Department of Organizational Behavior, Weatherhead School of Management, Case Western Reserve University. pp.1-80

Lambert, R (2003). *Lambert Review of Business-University Collaboration.* London. HMSO

Lester, S & Costley, C (2010). Work based learning at higher education level: value, practice and critique. *Studies in Higher Education 35 (5), 561-575.*

Nixon I, Smith K, Stafford R, Camm S. (2006). Work-based learning: Illuminating the higher education landscape. Final report. York. Higher Education Academy.

Nixon I (2008). Work-based learning. Impact study. York. Higher Education Academy.

Pegg, A, Waldock, J, Hendy-Isaac, S, Lawton, R (2012). Pedagogy for employability. York. Higher Education Academy.

Robbins, Lord (1963). Higher Education: report of the Robbins Committee. London. HMSO

Sappington, T.E. (1984). Creating learning environments conducive to change: The role of fear/ safety in the adult learning process. *Innovative Higher Education 9 (1), 19-29*

Scherer, K. R., & Tran, V. (2001). Effect of emotion on the process of organizational learning. In Dierkes, M., Berthoin-Antal, A., Child, J. & Nonaka, I. eds. *Handbook of organizational learning and knowledge* Oxford, UK: Oxford University Press. (369-394).

Yorke, M. & Knight, P. (2006). Learning and Employability (series one). Embedding employability into the curriculum. York. Higher Education Academy.

Chapter Five
The Specialist's Perspective
Patrick Smith

Introduction

In Chapter Three we discussed the range of elements which comprise the specialist role. This chapter focuses on the specialist's role within a sector-specific programme and is based on the reflections of three prominent members of the event and security sector who contribute to work-based learning programmes offered by an institution in the south east of England. Two of the interviewees are themselves graduates of work-based programmes, from Foundation Degree to Master's Degree levels, whilst the third is acknowledged as a foremost practitioner, thinker and writer within the event management sector.

During the summer of 2012, these practitioners took part separately in semi-structured interviews which were then transcribed, coded and analysed for the purposes of revealing the specialist's perspective. To offer further elaboration and a degree of triangulation, this chapter also incorporates a number of examples of recorded feedback from participants on and contributors to work-based programmes. In all cases respondents have approved the resulting text.

A decision was taken not to focus the interviews on the five meta-categories identified in our research with facilitators outlined in Chapter Seven. We felt that the imposition of such a structure might constrain and even distort responses and were eager to secure the respondents' independent perceptions of the roles that they had been fulfilling over recent years, expressed in their own terms.

The interviewees were asked to recall and comment upon the role they played as specialists, identifying what they felt were significant aspects, which were then pursued through additional questioning and prompting. Not surprisingly perhaps, the responses clustered around the following topics between which there was a certain amount of spillage. These were:

- the specialist's role in facilitation
- the challenges of participation in formal education
- the learning process
- the need for active involvement in learning.

Learning in the Round: the specialist's role

All three respondents emphasised the importance of identifying and relating to the participants' needs and purposes, of getting to know them and of establishing a rapport and a climate within the workshop which encouraged participation. Specialist A noted that:

> *"...you have to look at a slightly broader picture. You have to look at what the learner wants out of it."*

Specialist C makes a similar point, before going on to consider his role in creating a learning environment that promotes engagement with learning:

> *"What is it that they are looking to get from the workshops? You know, in terms of the material, the subject matter ... there's this environment where I can get these people to start thinking about their workplace, their responsibilities."*

Specialist C went on to amplify what he meant by the phrase 'this environment' in relation to creating conditions in which the participants felt able to open up and to engage in the learning process:

> *"...it's creating the right kind of setting, the right kind of atmosphere within the workshop (so) that people feel they're part of it."*

The prominence of the three specialists within the event management industry means that they are viewed with a certain amount of respect by participants, not least because they are practising managers. However each of them was at pains to downplay their roles and positions in order to establish links with the participants and to create common ground, as evidenced by Specialist A:

> *"And I was exactly the same as them. I had to learn by experience. When I first started, you know, I would put in a plan and I would put in the flow rate ... the pedestrian flow rate and then they (the participants) would ask me all the time, 'How do you know that?' And I'd say, 'Because I stood at the gate with a clicker and I counted it.'"*

The specialist serves to fulfil a number of other related roles, most notably those of resource, mediator and poser of questions. In many respects they are fulfilling a knowledge brokerage role, a topic to which we will return in Chapter Ten. Specialists are often seen as a walking resource, the living repositories of event management history, not a role which Specialist A is eager to fulfil, feeling that his role is to elicit more up-to-date examples and experiences from the participants:

> *"It's tricky because you've got the experience, but obviously the older you get the more distance you'll be coming from. It's no good me talking about what I did with the Osmond Family in 1974, or the Stones in the Park, they can get something from that, but the something, the thing they can get out of it is to see things have changed, how things are now."*

The response implies an interesting distinction from the pedagogic practice of the facilitator in the work-based learning process who might well be more concerned that the participant is able to identify underlying *principles* and traits which replicate across different contexts, rather than specific *examples* which are context-specific. Nevertheless, Specialist A also perceives an element of mediation and translation across contexts in his own role:

> *"So, you are acting as a translator, a middle-man, a mediator…"*

The centrality of pertinent case-studies and examples as a tool of the specialist was patent from the data set. Having established that rapport, along with those conditions in which participants felt able to engage in workshop activities, sharing their knowledge, and their ignorance, the specialist can then begin to present case-studies, incidents and 'near misses' for examination and challenge encouraging critical reflection on the part of the participants. Specialist B describes how:

> *"I look for live examples in workshops now and I try to get them to think about what they're facing … so they can go further and do their jobs better…to get their mind-set into the actual event that's coming up saying 'What would you consider? What do you need to think about? How will you consider it, what points do you need to consider?'"*

If the resulting discussion and analysis by participants does indeed achieve the desired level of criticality, so begins a process of 'role shifting' and collaborative learning as discussed in Chapter Three. In that chapter we noted the mutuality and reciprocity of learning between the respective actors, and the specialists were also quick to acknowledge that they too benefitted from the workshops. Specialist C:

> *"I think what you just called the mutuality of learning is really important because that's what gives the participants the confidence to engage. You know they don't hold back. They see themselves as equal and what you are is a pool of knowledge, you're a resource that they're reaching into … and that makes me think, that makes me, y'know, rethink what I know, how I'd do things … But you know it's working when they actually start to ask you questions that actually make you think."*

Specialists are aware of their own development and the need to provide information and insights which are demonstrably valid and workable, as Specialist B notes:

> *"I am very conscious of what I am telling them … it's basically, they're going to hold me to almost everything that I say, so I have to make sure I research the stuff, that I know it. And that takes time."*

Additionally, the interviews revealed an element of specialist awareness of their progression and development as facilitators and mediators of learning. Specialist C reports a development in his pedagogical style and approach which evokes Prosser and Trigwell's (1999) account of the development from a more teacher-centred conception of teaching to a more learner-centred facilitative and interpretative style. He felt keenly:

> *"I think when I first started, it was more about me standing, you know, more about me telling as opposed to explaining. And then it developed into more about explaining and creating the scenarios so that people could participate, and then move on."*

The use of questioning and challenging are indicative of a stage reached in the learning arena as Specialist C goes on to outline:

> *"(It) allows people to think and feel that to challenge something is not wrong, if you're challenging it out of reason, you know. And it's often about understanding the other person - the other party's views and their approach to something."*

And seemingly the confidence gained can transcend the classroom and find expression in other settings as Specialist B describes:

> *"The difference that made was ... you know, I could sit in a boardroom, or I could sit in a meeting with somebody more senior and challenge them in the right way. It wasn't (being) critical, it was constructive. And that's quite powerful, to change somebody's ability to go from a passive participant to somebody who can actually improve the workplace, or challenge the norms ... that's a by-product of the workshop experience."*

This notion of the potential benefits of unforeseen, even unintended outcomes or by-products through the examination of scenarios, case studies and events, and their potential for developing and consolidating both so-called 'soft' skills (Boyce et al, 2001) and higher order skills of analysis (Kreber, 2001) is a recurring theme in the Learning in the Round process.

Specialists then share many of the same interests and concerns as facilitators in terms of ensuring that they create conditions of trust, that they listen and observe the reactions and behaviours of participants and respond to them, and that they ensure that their material is accurate and up-to-date.

Specialist B referred to feeling the need to "research the stuff" and of interrogating his experience along the lines of:

> *"'Maybe they're missing things' and then (you ask yourself) 'Did I refer to that? Did I give it enough weight?' So then you need to take a step back and think 'Am I making the right links?' So, I am self-analysing."*

Assessment represents a perennial challenge to educators, be they experienced facilitators, or specialists involved in advising on participants' assignments. The following conversation between the interviewer and Specialist B serves to illustrate. When asked to describe his experience of assessing, Specialist B replied:

> *"Painful!" (Laughter) "It's a time-consuming business. I mean, you can kind of dread it coming around, even the little bit that I do. Yet, in a strange way, you learn a lot about the learner and the programme. But the main thing is fitting it in – I have to run a business at the same time."*

Specialist A summed up his response with the words:

> *"It's hard. You're making judgements about people – about their work and its value. It feels like there's nothing to hang on to, nothing to peg it onto."*

The challenge of entering formal education

Entering formal education represents a considerable challenge and transition for those whose background and experience have sometimes brought them little positive contact with formal learning. Lacking that cultural capital which those who have enjoyed success at school and in tertiary education wear so lightly, the shadow cast by the college, both literally and metaphorically is difficult to comprehend.

Specialist A outlines a typical biography for those in event management:

> *"I think you have to kind of draw a picture of the crowd safety person. It would probably be a person who left school without too many qualifications, probably none at all ... drifted into a job as a part-time occupation to earn a few pounds and then stayed on, and on ... and has gone up the ladder, if you like, because that person has a bit more common sense, a bit more brain than the next one so he became a supervisor or a manager."*

Having left school at the age of 15, Specialist B joined the army before migrating into the nascent event management sector in which he subsequently built up a major company. He eventually undertook a series of qualifications in the higher education sector culminating in a Master's Degree. As such, he is ideally placed to appreciate the challenges which confront those with little or no academic experience upon entering education as mature students; and as such he is ideally suited to act as a specialist whose knowledge of the challenges of tertiary education derives from direct and painful experience:

> *"Like I say, you learn as you go along the way and you make mistakes as you develop ... and it's the same with the path of academia, you know. I found it very difficult, and I still find it difficult to put into words what I actually think, I know what I am talking about, I can stand in a classroom and talk about it, but actually saying 'Right. How do I write that down? How do I write it in the way that it needs to be written, to be clear? How do I write it in a way where people can actually understand it and relate to it, and actually learn from it?' That's the difficult part."*

Formal post-secondary education is like a foreign country to such participants; they know neither the language, nor the customs: everything is different and they react with apprehension, suspicion and fear, as Specialist A notes:

> *"Basically, a lot of them are frightened of academia. They don't understand the language and they say 'Oh no. I can't do that.' You know, the old shutters go up straight away."*

The fear of exposing one's ignorance, particularly in front of one's peers, can act as a serious barrier to learning and the role of the facilitator working in collaboration with the specialist is to move beyond this constraint as Specialist A emphasises:

> *"They're not going to ask because they'll think 'I'm stupid' ... but then I'll find out the rest of the class don't know the answers either ... But once they get into it, they kind of see things in a language that they can understand and they can work with that, then it all becomes clearer."*

Specialist C makes a similar point about the importance of exposure and of making mistakes – of creating the conditions in which learning involves participants 'having a go' (Crawshaw, 2008):

> *"Getting people to be comfortable is allowing them to expose their ignorance, because it's all about learning from your mistakes ... allowing people to develop so that they don't make the same mistake twice. So you want them to think a bit differently ... but you can't make them feel inadequate because they've got it wrong. They have to make mistakes."*

'Thinking a bit differently' is an aspect of formal education practice that we will return to shortly, however before that we would like to turn to the issue of ignorance and the need to consider and discuss repeatedly until 'the penny drops.' Specialist A outlines a familiar situation:

> *"'Oh yeah' they'll say, 'I've got it.' But they haven't. You question them, you get them to show you and it's clear that they haven't got it ... and it's your job – I mean these guys are dealing with people in situations which could be dangerous – they've got to be sure. So you make them do it again and again and then they'll say 'Ah, now I've got it.' Then you can sit back for a minute."*

One of the tasks of tertiary education is that of developing critical and analytical thinking, of delving below the surface in order to identify assumptions and the reasoning behind those assumptions, in order to consider different possibilities and interpretations – in short of getting participants to 'Think a bit differently.'

In Chapter Three we presented a simple model of the three stages of Learning in the Round, noting that, initially participants' knowledge is largely tacit and that it needs to be accessed and realised in order to become amenable to critical collective examination. Developing the ability to accommodate and evaluate different and possibly even contradictory viewpoints enables participants to reach reasoned decisions, to make explicit that which was formerly tacit and to discuss it with others. It is not unusual in workshops for the following instance to occur as reported by Specialist A:

> *"... these people learn by experience, they could look at a crowd and say 'Well, you know, we should do something about that situation over there because that's going to turn nasty.' But if you ask 'Why?' they wouldn't be able to give you an answer ... at the end of a workshop they should be able to come out of it and say*

> *'I understand now why we have queue theory. I've been using queue theory for years. I didn't know I was doing it.'"*

Specialist B speaking about the importance of self-reflection poses the question 'Why is this process done?' and answers it as follows:

> *"It's like that single and double loop thinking stuff." (Argyris & Schon, 1978)*
> *"You start to take a different learning curve, you start to recognise different processes and that's the one thing I would say that academic [study] has done, it broadens the knowledge ... you start to look at things in a different way. And you can't do it overnight."*

Notions of learning

Arguably, one of the most invigorating and stimulating rewards for all concerned in the Learning in the Round process is that 'Eureka' or 'Meercat' moment when a participant takes hold of an idea and truly apprehends it. participants, specialists and facilitators have all referred to such moments when, it seems, the confines of the classroom and workshop have been transcended. This instance of apprehension may happen as a flash of insight, or may be more protracted. In Bakhtin's (1981) terms it is a process of 'appropriation' in which a concept, or word ceases to be:

> *"... half someone else's. It becomes 'one's own' only when the speaker populates it with his own intention, his own accent, when he appropriates the word, adapting it to his own semantic and expressive intention."*
> **(Bakhtin, 1981: 293)**

At this point undeniably a transformation occurs in which the learner perceives new vistas of understanding which reframe existing knowledge enabling the individual to re-interpret and extend it. "Light the blue touch paper and retreat" is an observation which is not uncommon for actors to experience in workshops and the grateful facilitator must determine whether to intervene in order to take and use that wave of energy, or whether to let it run its course within the group.

A seemingly natural consequence of such experiences is a redoubling of the individual's thirst for further knowledge and understanding – a thirst which can take them on extended journeys, even across continents as Specialist A recalls:

> *"We had somebody from Norway, I think he was, and there was a Brazilian guy who was talking about a problem he'd had. And then the Norwegian guy came in to the conversation and it was obvious from the conversation that he knew quite a lot about it. And I said, "Well, how did you know about what happened there." And he said, "Well, I was there. I went there." And then I said, "You mean, you went to Brazil to find out?" And he said, "Yeah.""*

We referred earlier in this chapter to participants learning from mistakes made and of the need for facilitators and specialists to create the conditions in which participants are able to share insights and experiences in order to make explicit those tacit understandings and assumptions which underpin their actions. The following interaction recollected by Specialist A is a common example of this process at work:

> *"A guy talks about an episode at an event – it was about people being searched going into a gig – so, he's telling it and before he can finish someone else in the group says 'Yeah, that happened to me' and the first guy says 'So, what did you do?'" and at that point you let them get on with it, it's a matter of sorting out what they mean, what they're actually saying ... and then they all pitch in."*

Successful workshops are replete with examples of peer learning of this nature at work, however the process can extend way beyond a particular moment in time at a workshop as the cohort assumes naturally their role in sharing information and thereby facilitating learning. Again Specialist A:

> *"... people are coming from countries all around the world and they are all able to access their computer and get involved. They also are talking to each other and then they start using this social network stuff, on Facebook, and things like that, and they are swapping their bits of video from YouTube and newspaper reports of incidents, something like that. So, if something happens in Brazil, you'll hear about it. If something happens in Germany, they'll send you the video. So, it's the learning they get from each other, but it's a different way of learning and then eventually, they will learn on the academic level, we can steer them towards how to write that paper, that assignment."*

The sharing of information and experiences starting with the 'That happened to me' 'Yeah, what did you do?' initiates the analytical phase in which participants consider their actions in comparison with those of their peers and begin to appreciate that in any situation a range of possible actions and solutions might exist. This process of analysis through discussion will require participants to present the reasoning behind their actions and those assumptions upon which their actions are based, thus fulfilling one of the functions of tertiary education, that of developing critical and analytical capabilities. Specialist B provides an illustration:

> *"... they start to use their own circumstances, their own situations and the actions could be 180 degrees spread, different. So they have to support their different methods, their approaches. And at first it can seem like they're talking Swahili to each other, because (they) couldn't relate to what they (the others) were saying."*

Specialist C illustrates the same process at work, emphasising the importance of what Schon (1987) terms 'giving the kid reason' or, at the very least taking time to tease out what the participant is trying to articulate:

> *"When you talk about the breadth of diversity (of opinions), the key to me is that everybody's point of view is relevant. So never, ... nobody can ever say something is not relevant. There's something to be extracted out of what anybody says, and, you know, what you want to do is, then, to root it out, to expand on that one little element."*

Specialist B echoes this notion of 'giving reason' in order to draw out what participants are trying to say:

"You have to look up and try and work out where they are coming from."

In the foregoing discussion practitioners will recognise evidence of the Kolb (1984) cycle at work and having illustrated how concrete experience is manifested in workshops, along with the need for ready application to the workplace of freshly developed conceptual understandings, we will turn now to the often neglected area of reflection. Given the action-centred nature of security and event management it is not surprising that this should be a neglected area of learning. However for Specialist B reflection represented a significant aspect of the personal learning journey, one which he was then at pains to encourage and support in participants in workshops:

"I think it sort of brought a lot of reflection into play. Self-reflection. "Why is this process done, like this?" Like the stuff on single loop and double loop thinking. You start to understand things in different way. You start to recognise different processes. You sit there and listen to what is being said and think, 'Yeah. I can relate that back to what I'm doing.' You then start to analyse and reflect and write things down. And I think that's the process that you know slowly I've been doing over the last sort of two or three years."

Active involvement in learning

Without exception the specialists agreed that they preferred and relied on developing a climate of relations in workshops which encouraged discussion and made use of active learning methods. Specialist B's view is representative of the specialists' views and he is emphatic about the limitations of traditional teaching methods and the need for involvement, a position which has been accepted in theoretical terms field of education, but less often realised in practice:

"I don't think lecturing all the time would work. Putting a PowerPoint presentation on the screen for the whole day ..." (sighs and gestures to indicate the futility of the approach) – "... by 11:00 o'clock, you might as well be talking to the wall, (they're) sleeping people, brain-dead people. I find that one of the methods I try to use a lot is participation. I think active participation within the classroom encourages them to think, encourages them to respond. It gets them to start using their grey matter and they might actually become involved and learn more,(so) the way we're doing the work-based learning I should say, it was small pieces, different people, talking about reality."
(See Mazur, 1996, Seeler at al, 1994)

Group work, case studies, incidents – critical or otherwise, 'near-misses' and scenarios, along with table-top exercises, video-clips are all used to stimulate discussion and focus attention on identifying possible options, actions, strategies and the subsequent deployment of resources. We will return to the topic of learning methods in Chapter Nine as the successful

Management briefing in the event arena – work-based learning in action.

use of such methods depends upon close cooperation between specialists and facilitators. For the present however we are eager to emphasise the importance, stressed across the data set, of the participant's active involvement in workshop activities.

A recurring metaphor referred to by the specialists is that of a journey in which all the workshop actors are involved. Specialist A:

> *"You're there to help them make sense of it ... what I would see my role then is to guide them along the route."*

This idea of guiding and accompanying the participants on that journey of learning was also referred to by Specialist B:

> *"I know it's difficult." (learning on formal education programmes). "I've done it. It's hard. It's getting your head into different places. The one thing I've learned in academia is you have to be able to support practical knowledge with evidence and we're not used to doing that. We don't do that. So I see what I'm doing there is kind of walking alongside with them – letting them make mistakes – being there."*

Conclusions

In this chapter we have tried to let the specialists speak for themselves about the experience of Learning in the Round. Readers, no doubt, will have been struck by the similarities between the respective roles of facilitator and specialist, and to some extent, the participants themselves.

It has been our experience that the most successful cohorts and programmes are those in which a sense of a community of learners and practitioners is established. This is evidenced by the commitment demonstrated in workshops along with those contacts and communications between and outside workshops between the actors involved. An additional positive outcome from this growing sense of community is that participants from previous cohorts serve firstly as ambassadors for recruitment to such programmes, encouraging colleagues to enrol and secondly as specialists who are willing to contribute to subsequent programmes: a virtuous cycle of development.

The data from the three discrete interviews can only indicate some initial bearings in documenting the experiences and perceptions of specialists facilitating work-based learning programmes, but the initial findings are suggestive and are corroborative of a view of Learning in the Round, in which role-shifting between actors is key and in which all the players are immersed in a sustained and particular form of pedagogy. What also emerges from the data is a sense of how the process of Learning in the Round supports the specialists in developing their own conceptions of pedagogic practice, the available evidence being that their engagement in facilitation enables them to build the more 'developed' (Prosser and Trigwell, 1999) or student-centred (Ramsden, 2003) conceptions of teaching that have been shown to correlate with high quality learning outcomes. Specialist C refers to just such a process of building a learning community and evinces that intuitive instinct of the learner-centred facilitator – the instinct to step back when appropriate and let the process of peer learning take its course:

> *"It's always a good time in those good, healthy exchanges of views and, you know, they don't need you then. You know, it shows that it's on the right track and it's working ... They're not really (needing you) ... they're actually talking to each other then. And it's about them anyway; it's not about you."*

References

Argyris, C. & Schon, D. (1987). *Organizational learning: A theory of action perspective.* Reading, Mass. Addison Wesley.

Bakhtin, M. M. (1981). The dialogic imagination. Austin, TS. University of Texas Press.

Boyce, G. Williams, S. Kelley, A & Yee, H. (2001). Fostering deep and elaborative learning and generic (soft) skills development: the strategic use of case studies in accounting education. *Accounting Education. 10. (1). 37 – 60.*

Crawshaw, M. (2008). How do adult learning theories relate to reflective practice? York. University of York.

Kolb, D. (1984). Experiential Learning: Experience as the Source of Learning and Development. New York. Prentice Hall.

Kreber, C. (2001). Learning experientially through case studies? A conceptual analysis. *Teaching in Higher Education. 6 (2). 217 – 228.*

Mazur, E. (1996). Are Science lectures a thing of the past? Physics World.

Prosser, M. and Trigwell K. (1999). Understanding Learning and Teaching: The Experience in Higher Education. Buckingham. Open University and SRHE.

Ramsden, P. (2003). Learning to Teach in Higher Education. (2nd ed). London. Routledge.

Schon, D. (1987). Educating the reflective practitioner. American Educational Research Association. Washington. DC.

Seeler, D, Turnwald, G. & Bull, K. (1994). From Teaching to Learning: Part III. Lectures and Approaches to Active Learning. *Journal of Veterinary Medical Education. 21 (1).*

http://scholar.lib.vt.edu/ejournals/JVME/V21-1/Seeler1.html

Chapter Six
The Participant's Perspective
Teresa Moore

Introduction

This chapter looks at the experiences of three participants who have been involved in a range of work-based learning provision, each coming from different backgrounds and being at different stages of their careers and education.

Throughout this chapter the definition of work-based learning used is broad, encompassing a variety of experiences which have incorporated learning in a work place environment. It is based upon Raelin's notion that:

> *"Work-based learning expressly merges theory with practice, knowledge with experience. It recognises that the workplace offers as many opportunities for learning as the classroom."*
> **(Raelin, 2008: 2)**

Furthermore the conception of work-based learning referred to here acknowledges Raelin's three 'critical elements' of the work-based learning process, namely that:

- it views learning as acquired in the action and is task-related
- knowledge creation and use is a social and collective activity
- learners develop a learning to learn mind-set.

Thus we consider short work placements of a few months duration as creating opportunities for work-based learning and have not adopted the QAA's (2011) tight definition of the concept, which specifically excludes placements and internships which are not mentored or otherwise formally based in the curriculum. We suggest that this definition tends to perpetuate the notion that learning and work are two separate activities which need to be bridged by mentors or other such facilitators. The view has been taken that work-based learning can take many forms which do not necessarily have to involve structured projects or supervision, but where, in these less formal settings, equally valid learning experiences can occur.

The three participants selected for interview were deliberately chosen to reflect a range of experiences at different stages of careers, work experience and learning. The aim was to determine whether there were common themes across their experiences and also whether there were any significant differences.

The chapter looks at how those industries where work-based learning can be particularly effective are often industries undergoing a process of professionalisation. The nature of professionalisation is explored and particular reference made to the music industry which is the focus of the programmes of study of all three of the interviewees.

The idea of learning as a journey and the importance of reflection are examined in some detail as is the notion of employer expectations in work-based learning.

The interviewees

A semi-structured interview approach was adopted. Interviews were recorded and the resultant transcript coded to identify recurrent themes both within and across the three interviews. The view was taken that the interview represents more a journey ranging across experiences, rather than an interrogation by means of predetermined themes. Each participant was interviewed about their experiences and encouraged to reflect on the form of their individual learning.

Participant A, a full time student on a three year undergraduate programme (BA Hons Music Management) undertook a series of short-term work placements in different types of organisations ranging from a major corporation to a small independent record label. She also managed operations at the University's in-house music label, MC9 Ltd. MC9's purposes and intended role in learning will be outlined later in this chapter. The degree programme Participant A studied is itself significant as it is one of a breed of highly vocational courses now available to students where the teaching and facilitation staff represent both significant and relevant industry experience, alongside academic qualifications and capabilities. The significance of such courses was noted by Tribe & Kemp as early as 1999 in an article which celebrated the integration of both the academic and vocational aspects of music industry management programmes. Participant A demonstrated a maturity somewhat at odds with her comparative youth particularly in terms of her initiative and determination, but also in terms of the level of reflection that she brought to her learning experiences during work placements.

In contrast Participant B has worked in the music industry for over 20 years and, typical of many in the industry, has been running his own music business during that time. He had come back into education to study a Masters in Music and Entertainment Management on a part-time basis. Previously Participant B had started an undergraduate degree course straight after leaving school, but did not complete it having decided to follow his passion for music. As a consequence he had only a limited experience of higher education and has had to relearn how to study and also to develop confidence in his ability to engage with education.

Participant C is also studying on a Master's programme, but on a full-time basis having worked for local government for the last six years, prior to which he had graduated with a first degree. He has continued to work alongside his Master's studies both for local government and also by managing his own band. His reason for seeking a Master's qualification was to help him pursue his dream of progressing further in the music industry. Participant C has had experience of full time education at the higher education level previously and therefore is more comfortable with the demands and practices associated with postgraduate study. Furthermore he has re-entered education with the view that it has increasing value in the workplace as the industry professionalises itself and can provide a platform for his career ambitions.

The music industry

At this stage it is appropriate to consider the current nature of the music industry as all three participants are studying Music Management qualifications. This is significant as the music industry, along with many of the newer industries, such as crowd safety management and event management are in the process of seeking to professionalise in terms of workforce qualifications and development, along with the establishment of accepted codes of practice and associated regulation.

The music industry had for many years resisted the notion of the value of formal education and qualifications. There are many still working in the industry, some in very senior positions who have achieved success without formal higher level qualifications. Until fairly recently these individuals have refuted the need for a more formal education structure and career progression pathways. Their direct work-based experience, in its loosest interpretation, has been the primary means of learning about the business and climbing the career ladder within the more corporate end of the sector, and of carving out successful business careers as entrepreneurs. It is worth noting that, like Participant B, some 80 per cent of those working in the music and entertainment industries are either self-employed or working for Small to Medium-sized Enterprises (SMEs) where investment in education has been seen as a luxury, perhaps even as an indulgent distraction, rather than a necessity.

It is worth noting that in our experience this view is changing, perhaps as a result of the fundamental changes that have occurred in the music industry over the past decade, such as those brought on by the advent of digitisation. Slowly but surely the need for a more sophisticated and educated workforce has been recognised even by the most successful entrepreneurs as they grapple with the complexities of ever-evolving business models, advances in technology and consequent changes to the structure of the industry. Increasingly even SMEs are approaching higher education institutions looking for students and graduates to fill an expanding range of employment opportunities.

Industry professionalisation

For some industries the recognition that they need to professionalise has emerged quite recently. Professionalisation has manifested itself in a number of ways including an acceptance that formal qualifications and taught courses can make available a significant level of knowledge and training which provides those entering the industry with skills that "on the job training" might not achieve alone. It is worth looking here at this process of professionalisation which is currently occurring.

The music industry prospered for a long time using what worked well in conditions which were relatively stable. Whilst there were changes in technology, they were still around a physical product such that existing business models, along with the behaviours, values and assumptions which underpinned them, continued to remain viable. The situation was one in which changes were incremental thus making it possible for the industry to flex and adapt to changes in technologies, such as the development of the cassette tape followed by that of the CD. Problems occurred as soon as changes in technology moved from the incremental to the fundamental. Formats became digital, conditions in which those pre-existing business models, attitudes and values were stretched to the point where they no longer operated effectively and, indeed, impacted significantly and negatively on profitability. It took the industry some time to realise that it needed original and fresh approaches and ways of thinking which were radically different and more sophisticated than those of the past.

It was at this point that the realisation dawned that there was a need for a developed and explicit body of underpinning knowledge, which until then only existed empirically and tacitly. This is not dissimilar to the position of other industries already referred to which have had to face a variety of new challenges. A professionalisation process capable of reflecting on and dealing with these challenges is necessary to develop an industry to the point where it can embrace change, creating new business models, practices and behaviours and allowing the industry to exploit fully the new technologies, ideas and associated regulatory changes. Whilst causal links are yet to be proven, it is true to say that a shift in view by industry concerning the importance and role of education and training has emerged alongside these changes. There is now a consistent demand from employers for individuals who have the relevant vocational qualifications, education and training. This trend towards professionalisation can be seen in many other formally vocational industries such as dance teaching, security and policing, whilst occupations such as nursing are well down the road towards consolidating a professional identity.

These occupations are all in the process of mapping and attempting to secure for themselves discreet areas of specialised practice which in time will involve the creation of a structure for self-regulation. The problem is that there is little by way of a developed body of knowledge underpinning this professionalisation process and as a consequence knowledge is drawn eclectically from a range of sources. The resulting knowledge base is both wide-ranging and trans-disciplinary in nature and, as such, is not necessarily fixed, stable or indeed exclusive to the industry. In these circumstances knowledge tends to be the product of a range of contributions and is co-created.

Miller (1998) outlines the process of the social construction of professional identity in relation to osteopathy, however it is evident that in a similar way the industries referred to in this chapter are undergoing a process of constructing a professional identity of their own with all the accommodations to circumstance and associated compromises that are perceived to be required as part of the professionalisation process. And, as with Miller's osteopaths, these industries are responding to changes taking place within the environment in which they operate – changes in technology, public perceptions and agendas, or in the case of the crowd safety industry in response to significant disasters, their subsequent investigation, reporting and consequent legislation.

The foregoing illustrates just how complex is the nature of professionalisation. On the face of it traditional characterisations of professions, such as those embodied in trait approaches, emphasise the significance of the possession of certain features or traits, such as established codes of practice, ethical codes and a discreet body of knowledge over which practitioners have a virtual monopoly. Such professions are typically self-regulating, as with the legal, medical and accountancy professions; conditions which carry with them associated notions of the relationship between the professional and his/her client in terms of distance and objectivity.

In order to enter a particular community of professional practice, significant training and qualifications are required which, once achieved, provide those who are members with a degree of confidence and status. Importantly qualified status also gives those who engage with members of these professions a similar confidence and reassurance in the practitioner's competence and levels of expertise.

In contrast to the trait approach to professions and professional identity, the symbolic approach to professionalisation emphasises a range of what might be termed political processes involving the careful management of identity through communication, influence and negotiation. Miller's (1998) article amply illustrates the twists and turns which brought osteopathy from folk practice – avowedly in direct opposition to the formal medical world based on emerging scientific principles – to a respectable profession, a process, according to Fine quoted by Miller by means of which:

> *"Through occupational rhetoric, workers justify their work and explain to themselves and to their public, why they feel what they do is admirable and/or necessary.*
> *(Miller, 1998: 1739)*

For further illumination on these issues, Wilensky (1964) provides an amusing outline of the professionalisation process and the apparently universal desire to achieve professional status whilst, more recently, Eraut's work (1994 & 2009) illustrates comprehensively the means and stages of professionalisation. For emergent professions, however, that level of assurance and confidence resident within the traditional professions is absent and it has to be developed alongside the underpinning knowledge base and educational framework. As a consequence, in the early stages members of these communities will still be uncertain and insecure in their knowledge base, an attitude which manifests itself in reactions of scepticism, distrust and defensiveness. However, as Participant B reflected about his industry experience in relation to his experience of returning to education:

"What I knew still has a value as long as I keep reassessing it."

Participant B is typical of the old industry without qualifications, but conversely he is also a representative example of the new and emerging ideas and approaches which illustrate an industry beginning to realise what is required.

MC9

At Buckinghamshire New University we have developed a different route for providing work experience for our students. We have established a limited company which is run as a commercial enterprise. Students can engage with the business in a variety of roles to suit their interests. The business is managed and the students' work overseen by staff who are both industry professionals and academics. The aim of MC9 is to provide real-life experiences where students can discover or source talent, and get involved in the negotiation of legal contracts with real artists – contracts which are then signed to the music label arm of the business.

Participant A in particular became very involved in the day to day operation of MC9 finding the experience provided her with:

"... a formal practice and full understanding of how every aspect of the company works together, rather than in segments."

which had been her previous experience on the degree programme.

MC9 continues to provide opportunities for students to apply the theory learned in the classroom to the practical experience of working for a music business. The challenge for the staff involved in managing the company and the related learning opportunities for the students is to ensure that those who do become involved reflect upon their experiences and, as Participant A has done, take them back into the classroom to support and augment their studies and continue the cycle of learning.

Reflections on learning

On a number of occasions we have referred to the notion of metacognition and the associated notion of cumulative learning which is defined as:

> *"...the accumulation of knowledge over a lifetime and its application to the learning of new tasks."*
> *(Swarup et al, 2005: 1)*

We take Flavell's (1979) notion of metacognition as higher order thinking designed to control the cognitive processes engaged in thinking and acquiring knowledge, in short, 'knowing about knowing' being aware of the effectiveness of one's personal learning strategies.

From the perspective of an undergraduate who had only experienced formal learning, going into the workplace allowed Participant A to apply her knowledge and also to appreciate that organisations have interlinked departments and processes. Work-based learning can promote a more holistic form of learning unlike academic learning which tends to be in uniform segments or bite sized chunks (Hussey and Smith 2010), whether it is through individual modules or even different semesters. Participant A notes that:

> *"In Uni you kind of learn in segments, refine and redirect what you do, whereas it's actually all interlinked ... when you go into the workplace you find that it's actually a holistic approach."*

Work-based learning can provide an opportunity for these 'segments' to be brought together, in other words learning becomes a holistic experience enabling those taking part to see the bigger, more realistic picture.

In contrast, given his age and experience, Participant B's viewpoint is from the opposite standpoint. He has accumulated a lifetime's experience in the music industry which he is now bringing with him to formal education and he notes that:

> *"It's made me more aware and more conscious of the issues and helped me to better understand the whole debate ..."*

In this instance the debate that Participant B refers to is that of the extent of the impact of digitisation on business models and the consequent fundamental changes to the way business is done in his industry. In his case the formal learning is providing a structure which enables him to make sense of his experience: it is creating an environment in which he can reflect upon his knowledge and experience:

> *"So I think (the programme) has made me pay more attention, become more focused and seek to be better informed of situations that I thought I knew about, but perhaps was kidding myself as to how much I did actually know."*

Participant C refers to the notion of the academic programme imposing a structure to his experiences and directing him towards systematic study, whilst also encouraging him to think differently, to consider other options which the habitual demands of daily work might preclude:

"I think returning to academia has forced me to read and research a lot more around the subject. When you're working you kind of feel different parts of your brain working ... in academic, you feel other parts of your brain working. It's been very refreshing to go back and get thinking in a different mind-set ... it encourages you to think a bit more blue sky, outside the box 'What if we did it this way? What if we did it that way?'"

For Participant B something of the same process of recollection and re-evaluation has occurred as he engaged in and understood better the reflective process that is necessary for learning:

"It's made me challenge my own opinions and try to validate them through reading, through referencing, through listening"

MC9 provided the opportunity for a similar learning experience for Participant A and it is clear from her experience that this type of learning not only reinforces previous learning, but importantly serves to build confidence:

"In the third year I'm re-learning things that I learned in the first and second year and bringing them back together."

Participant B's view of learning and reflecting upon his experiences also fosters this broader, more holistic mind-set:

"It shouldn't just be working towards a particular module and then, "Well, that's done. Forget about that." I've seen that as I've gone into the second year, as I do the dissertation, I'm not abandoning what I did in the first year. I think there's a connection between the two things. And there's been development from what I did last year to this point."

Work-based experience provides participants with the opportunity to experience the business as a whole. MC9 specifically allowed Participant A to see:

"... the actual workings of a record label and how each department is interlinked with each other. You get formal practice and a full understanding."

All the respondents referred to the value of seeing the business as a whole and to the confidence and credibility they saw accruing from this capability as Participant C reports:

"The fact that you've done a degree, it advertises (that you) know about the bigger picture and how the whole industry works (and) you understand where you fit in within the entire industry."

We can see from the experiences of all three respondents that they have been able to reflect back on previous learning and have developed the ability to integrate this into what they are currently doing, whilst developing an understanding of the industry as a whole. Furthermore this process has sparked the desire to investigate and understand more, whether as a result of the classroom experience in Participant B's case, or as a result of learning in the workplace in Participant A's case, or both as in Participant C's experience.

Ripple effects of learning

The importance of positive reinforcement in relation to motivation has been an accepted feature of effective learning and teaching for many years. Learning begets more learning (Clayton et al, 2009; Clouder, 2009; Eraut, 2009) and, crucially as a by-product, increased confidence, along with a willingness to branch out, to 'have a go.' As Participant B notes:

> *"Learning spurred more learning. I wanted to find out more and did a course in digital media as a result of a session we did on the Master's".*

Participant B's experience within a programme was similar to Participant C's, although for him it was the driver to return to education. Participant C's experience of first taking an undergraduate degree followed by a period in the workplace, created a desire and realisation that he wanted to extend his learning in a specific area:

> *"I'm here because I want to learn more."*

Participant C acknowledges that on returning to education his motivation was different this time:

> *"I'm not here because I want to go out to the Students' Union and live the student life. I'm here because of the academic study and that's what I wanted to do."*

Participant A has acquired theoretical and conceptual knowledge which she has taken with her into the workplace and reinterpreted it in the light of her experiences there, whereas Participant B and Participant C's journeys have been in the opposite direction. Their learning started as largely experiential and entering higher education has required them to reinterpret their experiences in the light of theoretical and conceptual understandings. To view learning, however as unproblematic and uni-directional, in one direction or the other would be to over-simplify the process in operation. The learning is not a one-way process as the research demonstrated. Each of the interviewees found there to be a reciprocal process at work in which formal study helped them understand aspects of the work place and provided a frame of reference, whilst the experience gained in the work place had, as Participant B said "real value" when it came to their studies.

As Participant B illustrates:

> *"I think the two sessions on IP (Intellectual Property) were really interesting. It's made me more aware and more conscious of a lot of issues, – it's helped me better understand the industry debate on streaming."*

And Participant C:

> *"So just understanding things like how a contract works...how to handle yourself within a recording studio."*

The emerging significance and knowledge of the role played by social media and how it might effectively be integrated into an overall marketing strategy is a topic referred to by all three respondents, as Participant C illustrates:

> *"... things that I've learnt that are important within the industry, such as updating the social media profile, making sure you've got the merchandising resources out ... or who's chasing up the reviewers to come along to the gigs ..."*

The role of social media in promotion and marketing is something that Participant C refers to later on:

> *"It's immediately applicable. You can see how you relate that straight away to what you do as a manager of a band."*

This notion of reciprocity not only applies to the personal learning of the individual, but also to exchanges in the workplace, as Participant A Illustrates:

> *"... they (the employers) realised they could learn something from me."*

Expectations, practice and theory

Learning and experience are bounded by expectations by the employer, specialists and the participant (employee). One of the recurring issues concerning expectations is that of contradictory and/or unclear expectations on the part of the employer regarding the intern, as Participant C reflects:

> *"I think they offered the role in really good faith, but I don't think the nature of what they were doing ... they weren't in a position where they were clear about it."*

In cases where the employer regularly takes on interns or provides longer work placements, there tends to be an expectation that the participant knows little and is therefore not expected to be able fully to engage in the work place at other than the superficial level. Interns when they enter the workplace can find that in fact they have a greater knowledge of some aspects of the business than either co-workers or the employers realise: As Participant A commented:

> *"I think they had less expectations actually. I think they didn't realise that I knew as much as I did. But then they understood that I've learned about management contracts and I've seen management contracts and worked with management contracts and things with publishing as well. I know the ins and outs of publishing. At Company X, they didn't quite fully understand the fact that I actually knew. I do know a great deal about the industry even though, I suppose, it's quite naive. But I know how it works. I think they do not give you the best opportunities because they think, "Well, she's just a student. She's just here to get*

the experience". When, actually, I'd like to be seen as an employee, an equal in the company."

Increasingly vocationally-based courses which are led by industry professionals who are also academics provide the tools and contextual framework which focus on both the theoretical knowledge and its application within the industry. For example role play in contract negotiation is a method used to teach both the principles of contract negotiation and to approximate the practical issues and behaviours which students will find when they are required to negotiate real contracts in the workplace. Recently one of our students who had, prior to a work placement, complained that they couldn't see the point of the role play exercise, on return commented to the tutor that they had been required to negotiate a contract on their placement, and that:

"It was exactly like the role play exercise".

Once the student's knowledge from their course and their capabilities are discovered the employer will often entrust a greater responsibility to that individual which in turn allows them to capitalise upon their experience and to develop their knowledge and confidence further. Participant A again:

"I think, yeah. I think there were a few times especially at Companies X and Y I kind of shocked them with my knowledge that actually I do know about the industry. I just said a couple of things about different territories and different regulations. And they're like, "Oh, you do know about that thing." So, yeah."

Participant A's experience demonstrates that sometimes a student will go into the workplace knowing more than the employers about particular and often current aspects of the business, because the programme and tutors are themselves at the forefront of knowledge in these areas. Participant A illustrates:

"I did a few things about digital marketing. And they're a bit like, "Oh, right. Okay. So then, you might know a bit more than we do about that." So I was given those jobs to do."

It is possible that highly vocationally-focused programmes such as the one on which Participant A was studying, may help those going into the workplace move into communities of practice with greater ease as they already know some of the unwritten rules that govern entry into that community. This is an issue which was discussed in Chapter Two with reference to the work of Lave and Wenger (1991).

Expectations are not only the province of the employers in a work-based setting. An employee with many years of work experience can come into education and not expect that they will gain much from the experience. Thus the participant as mature student who has many years' experience in their chosen field may underestimate the value and potential benefits of a formal programme of study, as was the case with Participant B:

> *"I think the overall benefit in the master's is it brings you up to speed with a lot of issues and it should also motivate you to go forward and work further with them."*

Our experience on the Master's programme is that there can be a tendency amongst participants to expect that they already have the answers and that they will not be taught anything new, whereas what they find is that they are encouraged to step back from their experience and reflect critically upon it. And it is in this process of 'stepping back,' distancing themselves from the working environment, that the reflective process stimulates fresh insights requiring them to reconsider long-held opinions. At the same time the accelerating pace of change, particularly technological change, along with consequent legal and ethical implications inevitably will be new to the participant. Participant B illustrates this aspect:

> *"What was said to me when I started on the Master's was that I would know a lot of this stuff. And I was ... I didn't understand how that could be the case. And I was surprised for example, going through issues on Intellectual Property (IP). I've never spent a lot of time looking at IP or what it did to concern me. I knew of it, but like so many, I wasn't paying attention to it. As we started to get drawn into it, I realised that I had been involved in those situations of unknowingly protecting copyright, or unknowingly protecting some of these recorded property rights and not understanding that process.*
>
> *(As a result) I find myself engaging in the sessions in a slightly different way. What I was trying to do in the sessions was share the experience I'd had and the situations that I find myself in. Partly to (get) involved in any discussion that the tutor was starting, but also to share it with the group and get the dialogue going.*
>
> *I've always found that if I could come up with examples of situations that I've been in and it helped to get away from the theory and put it into more practical terms. And I find myself, as I went through the course, these things were happening. I wouldn't call it easy because I found getting back to the process of study hard, but actually, the content, the knowledge was there. It was how to reference it and turn what perhaps had been opinion and what you thought you knew, into validated fact."*

What Participant B is referring to here is the process of learning through reflection on practice. This involves developing what is tacit knowledge, by bringing it to the surface, making it explicit and then subjecting it to scrutiny both by the individual and the group, a recurring element in Learning in the Round.

Encouraging reflection on work-based practice

So theory is realised as informed practice and in order to capitalise on this, reflection is a key component of the process. Again, Participant B illustrates:

> *"And (it is) what I said earlier that it's made me challenge my own opinions and to try and validate them through reading, through referencing, through listening.*

So, I'm hoping that some of what you know glibly, and I know I'm not alone in this, people from the music industry would walk in and say, "Yeah, I can teach. I know that stuff." And then you give them a theory and it's like, "Well, you know, I've never had to do any of this. We don't do all of that." You know, and you need it brought back to yourself – how that theory applies to what you've done. You might have been doing it for a long time without realising it. But through reading the theory and understanding it, it helps you to refine and redirect what you do. So, that has helped."

In terms of offering challenges to existing thinking and associated practices, Participant C's view was similar:

"I thought we would be doing the modules and I was hoping that it would challenge me more, which it has very much done. And it's just got me thinking, "Ah, yes, I forgot about that. I need to read more about that. Oh, that's a good idea. We could do that with the band.""

All of which demonstrates that there is transference between the learning that goes on in the classroom and the learning that goes on in the workplace, and vice-versa. But it is the process of reflection that is central to learning, helping individuals to put their experiences into context and further their ability to apply knowledge from whichever source.

Developing reflective practice as part of the path towards critical analysis and evaluation

Kolb (1984) and Cooper (1975) illustrate the process taking place as we move from experience and reflection on practice towards critical analysis and evaluation. The process can be summed up as one in which initial and habitual responses in the form of tacit theories, are identified, applied and adapted within the context that the individual finds themselves. This essentially metacognitive process then moves through the reflective stage where accessing and refining theoretical concepts in relation to practical experience occurs to emerge explicitly in the form of critical analysis and evaluation where a refining and focusing of what is learned is constructed before being applied afresh.

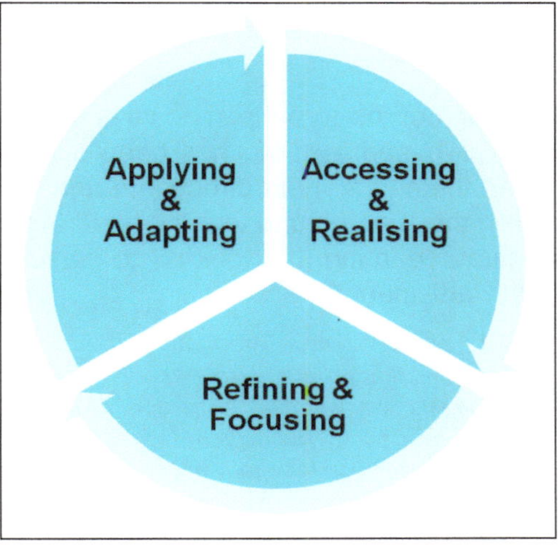

*Figure One. A simplified version of the learning cycle. (**Smith, 2011**)*

Conclusions

So what conclusions can be drawn about the participants' experiences of work-based learning?

It would seem that work-based learning has been particularly effective for the individuals interviewed in terms of realising, refining and applying their understandings and capabilities, for example by stimulating research and further independent study to address perceived areas of need. All three interviewees are working within changing contexts, both within their specific workplaces and roles, and within the broader industry as it seeks to gain recognition and achieve professional status.

The interviews reveal that learning is not a one-way process and that what is learned in the workplace is of value and informs existing theory, but also that what is learned in the classroom and workshop has real value in the workplace, particularly where the theory has already been grounded and earthed in a practice context. There is a constant interplay between the contexts of the workplace and the academy by means of which it is possible to generate considerable synergies of learning and development. Such is the case on many vocational courses where teaching staff have an industry background. This should not be taken to imply that staff without industry experience cannot effect this reciprocal application, but it cannot be denied that it is a feature of many successful vocational courses that the teaching staff have relevant industry experience and can readily contextualise the theory. This, in turn, allows participants such as Participant A to see how to apply the theory once they move into the workplace. Conversely, for Participant B and Participant C who have industry experience, it allows them to contextualise practical experience and provides a greater understanding of that experience and why they have done the things that they have done.

For each of the three interviewees that took part in the study the process of work-based learning has been a journey, but not a journey that has taken them in a linear direction, rather it has been an iterative process in which they have found that the work experience has prompted them to re-evaluate learning that took place earlier in their studies as was the case with Participant A:

> *"I think also, I mean, especially in third year, you're ... I'm learning that I'm bringing things back in from what I've learned the first year, because I suppose, along the way you think "First year, okay, it is just the first year, then second year, third year." But actually, when you get to the third year and even in the second year, you have to bring back everything you've learned from the first year and the second year. So I think it's quite, as a journey, I think you learn a lot more through it."*

And:

> *"I think I developed in MC9. I've got a lot more confidence and a lot more*

responsibilities as well ... I know the ins and outs of the company, the ins and outs of contracts. I know what to do and how to do it properly. And know who to contact and what areas to contact. And think if anyone has got problems, they can always come to me with confidence."

Or, as with Participant B where:

"I was off on a journey of music. Now it's the same with the study. You know, I'm finding you read in one piece, somebody references something else, the next thing you're spending hours to try to find out more about this text. And now I'm a member of The British Library, the Reading Room. That's great fun if you're hungry enough to go and explore it."

So, as Fox (1983) adroitly noted, Learning in the Round involves a journey which is undertaken with participants and peers, facilitators and specialists, a journey which engages participants in a continuous dialogue and as that journey proceeds the individual learns in the round.

References

Clayton, B. Beard, C. Humberstone, B. & Wolstenholme, C. (2009). The jouissance of learning: evolutionary musings on the pleasures of learning in higher education. *Teaching in Higher Education. 14 (4). 375 – 386.*

Clouder, L. (2009). 'Being responsible': students' perspectives on trust, risk and work-based learning. *Teaching in Higher Education. 14 (3). 289 – 301.*

Cooper, C. (1975). Theories of group processes. London. Wiley.

Eraut, M. (1994). Developing professional knowledge and competence. London. Falmer Press.

Eraut, M. (2009). How professionals learn through work. http://learningtobeprofessional, pbworks.com/ Date accessed, October 2009.

Flavell, J. (1979). Metacognition and cognitive monitoring. American Psychologist. 34. 906 – 911.

Fox, D. (1983). Personal theories of teaching. *Studies in Higher Education. 8 (2). 151 – 163.*

Hussey, T. & Smith, P. (2010). The trouble with higher education. London. Routledge.

Kolb, D. (1984). Experiential learning. New Jersey. Prentice Hall.

Lave, J. & Wenger, E. (1991). Situated learning: legitimate peripheral participation. Cambridge. Cambridge University Press.

Miller, K. (1998). The evolution of professional identity: the case of osteopathic medicine. Social Science & Medicine. 47 (11). 1739 – 1748.

Quality Assurance Agency. (2011). PMA 15 Code of Practice - Placement learning

Raelin, J. (2008). Work-based Learning. San Francisco. Jossey-Bass.

Smith, P. (2011). Personal communication.

Swarup, S. Mahmud, M. Lakkaraju, K. & Ray, S. (2005). Cumulative learning: towards designing cognitive architectures for artificial agents that have a lifetime. Department of Computer Science, University of Urbana-Champaign, Urbana. IL.

Tribe, J. & Kemp,C. (1999). The music industry management degrees: hitting the right note? *Journal of Vocational Education & Training. 51 (4). 521 – 536.*

Wilensky, H. (1964). The professionalisation of everyone. *The American Journal of Sociology. LXX (2). 137 – 158.*

Chapter Seven
The Facilitator's Perspective

Maurice Gledhill and Patrick Smith

Introduction

In this chapter we will set out the findings of a limited piece of research carried out with four experienced work-based learning facilitators. Each of these facilitators works on a range of conventional under- and postgraduate programmes comprising lectures, seminars, workshops and those electronic platforms which support classroom learning so that their observations often compare their experiences of teaching traditional programmes with the facilitation of work-based programmes.

We have referred previously in Chapter Three to the significant demands placed upon facilitators and specialists in accommodating the needs and demands of work-based participants, particularly in those areas which involve team work, collaboration and a trans-disciplinary orientation. Given the nature of academic specialisms and disciplinary allegiances those academics prepared to undertake the facilitation role as outlined previously are limited in number. Those who do accept the role find its challenges and rewards frustrating, often surprising and frequently stimulating.

In considering the facilitator role we are reminded of Hoyle's (1976) distinction between restricted and extended professionals; the former characterised by their focus on classroom activities and relationships, the latter by the broader context of learning and education. Whilst Hoyle's focus was on school teaching and assumed classroom performances being at the heart of the role, the situation with regard to tertiary education is complicated by the teaching-research divide. However as Trigwell et al (2000) demonstrate, a not dissimilar cycle exists for the higher education sector in which individuals can move from a classroom focus characterised by an awareness of the literature of student learning through systematic researching of classroom activities to the dissemination of the outcomes of research within the wider community of scholars.

Those who become successful facilitators of work-based learning appear to be individuals who find in the challenge of accommodating the distinctive needs of adult and part-time students something worthwhile, not least in terms of the need to respond flexibly and appropriately to needs and interests as they arise – they become adept at being light-footed in the classroom and workshop settings.

In the remainder of this chapter we will present our findings drawing on the responses of the facilitators.

Five meta-categories

Motivation

Under the general heading of motivation we identified the following four sub-categories in relation to mature work-based learners, namely that they:

- are self-motivated
- focus on strategic benefits
- have a marked work ethic, and
- have a wealth of experience.

Facilitator A was struck by participants' sense of purpose and direction:

"(They) come in having been established in their careers, so they've got much more focus, much more direction ... I think they care more." (A)

going on to note that:

"... they become much more engaged in their work than undergraduate students ... (they are) self-directed."

Furthermore mature students appear to appreciate how assignments consolidate learning and are not an imposition, as evidenced by Facilitator C:

"Because the types of assessments that we use are flexible, they can create their own work-based assessments and they don't actually know that they're doing it [learning], but they are ... Therefore they are more likely to do their assignment because it gives them value."

Facilitator B also reflects this notion of utility and value:

"I think they feel the fact that this is going to be useful to them ... to them it is not just doing it for the sake of filling in an assignment and completing the course ... It's because this is going to be useful ..."

The same facilitator emphasises the importance of linking assessment activities to practical and work-based concerns and issues:

"All their assignments are really much geared up around their workplace, it makes it a big difference because all (the) research projects that they do are around that theme that their employers have asked them to do or have encouraged them to do. So they have that sort of notion of utility. 'I'm doing this research because this is going to be useful to my workplace.'"

This same facilitator goes on to acknowledge those resources of experience that adult learners bring to the programme, but that they are sometimes unable or unwilling to value that experience:

"[They have] lots of work experience. Their expectation is that higher education is slightly different, they think it's a really, really difficult thing to achieve, you know, something very hard."

Echoing this sentiment Facilitator C states:

> *"Because to me, what work-based learning is, it's about enabling people with high levels of skill and involvement, and also, many years' experience, to be able to learn the underpinning theories and values that are within that process."*

Immediacy of application

Two major sub-categories emerged under this heading, each of which represents dilemmas and tensions whose resolution is often not straight forward.

Potential tensions between academic cultures and approaches, and the more pragmatic/outcomes-based cultures of the workplace, and difficulties associated with integrating new ideas and approaches which can run counter to a participant's immediate professional targets and needs.

Facilitator B recognises the differences between the worlds of work and the academy in terms of research:

> *"We expect a good understanding of sampling strategies and of research paradigms – quantitative and qualitative – those kinds of things. They don't necessarily fit with industry research, which might be as simple as 'I'm just going to go and ask a hundred people about this.'"*

Facilitator D in preparing and delivering sessions is at pains to make links between practice and theory:

> *"I would always bring in an area that relates to the workplace. So it doesn't matter how far-fetched it seems ... I think if they're learning a particular theory, you always bring it back to where that relates to the workplace, the implications that [it] has, what the problems might be."*

This process of linking theory and practice also involves entertaining and evaluating alternative and possibly conflicting opinions, as Facilitator D, teaching on a module concerned with vulnerable adults:

> *"So [it's] actually putting a different head on, thinking of different points of view. So one minute thinking of their being as a victim and their issues, the next minute thinking of it as being the facilitator and knowing the victim's perspective of what they would do. And then also by doing that, they not only saw the fact that some people have similar issues themselves, but they're happy to look at the same information from a number of different levels."*

Facilitator B indicates some of the problems in terms of expectations between institutions, participants and employers:

> *"When employees are driving the whole thing, then that's not a problem. I think that's good. But the problem comes when the employer doesn't understand the meaning of research, or finding the truth and they're interfering."*

Facilitator C refers to the potential barriers of habits and localised workplace practices and cultures that need to be surfaced and examined in terms of their appropriateness:

"... the norms and values created in that working environment have been done that way for so many years ... You have actually to engage and take those norms and values on – challenge them – so that people are not carried along in the same vein that they have been for many years."

Learning to learn is an inevitable consequence of learning new ideas, theories and approaches and becoming aware of their existing understandings about education and learning and what is being demanded of them is a necessary and occasionally difficult transition for the participant to make as Facilitator B notes:

"There are concepts and new terminology and (knowing) why this is important because some of them say, 'Why do I have to memorise things?' and I said, 'It's not about memorising. It's about starting to learn how to think and thinking is operating with concepts. Unless you know the meaning of the concepts, you cannot think.' So they understood that."

Managing conflicting demands and agendas

Conceptual categories such as those which we identified from the research initiative reported here have a tendency to elide one with the others. In the previous section we have outlined some of the tensions which can arise between employee, employers and academic staff. In this section we will focus more on the potential tensions and conflicts in terms of domestic agendas and time management such as those between the professional, academic and domestic, and those relating to time and task management.

Time and task management are perennial issues for the part-time adult learner; however often the very complexities and potentially conflicting responsibilities have enabled such learners better to manage their resources, as Facilitator B notes:

"They manage much better their time."

Some professional sectors require their employees to be able to travel abroad at short notice, a situation which creates a range of problems on the domestic and academic fronts, quite apart from maintaining continuity on the professional front. Participants from the military, event management and security industries are those most likely to be subjected to these challenges.

Attendance at workshops is the most immediate problem, though this can be overcome by participants joining subsequent cohorts on the same programme. The demand for facilitators tends to centre upon maintaining contact with participants and keeping them in touch with programme deadlines. Email and Skype have proved invaluable in alleviating the attendant difficulties and frequently assignments will appear through the ether from remote parts of the world.

Personnel from the security, military, close protection and disaster management fields are frequently required to travel abroad at short notice, a situation which can play havoc with assignment schedules. It has been our experience however that these conditions do not necessarily prevent participants from completing work; in some respects they appear to facilitate the submission of assignments. When asked, participants note that it is frequently the case when off-duty during a posting to a distant location, assignment preparation alleviates boredom by providing a sense of purpose and structure. There is only so much satellite television that can be absorbed before academic study starts to represent a diverting alternative. Two colleagues illustrate respectively:

> *"They (participants) often speak of carrying notepads with them in order to record ideas and observations they reach whilst carrying out their professional duties. Someone said to me 'It's easy enough to just make a note of something and then, later on, use it as a headline to remind you of what you were thinking.'*

> *"I was surprised at first to find out that they were using Facebook to talk to each other, firstly about assignments, y'know – 'What's he expecting us to do?' – that sort of thing, but as the course went on they were using it to swap experiences and how they related to what they were doing in the workshops."*

Facilitator C also refers to using Facebook to tune in to what participants are thinking and saying about the demands made by their programmes and their on-going observations. Maintaining contact outside the formal programmes of study becomes an important aspect of participant's time and task management as Facilitator B notes:

> *"The groups tend to be more homogenous ... they keep in touch and they engage in dialogue, and they learn from each other."*

Maintaining contact also indicates the extent of a cohort's commitment and sense of identity; there is little doubt that a strong sense of cohort identity contributes hugely to the success of those participants who comprise it. This feature plays a prominent role in the pedagogic relationship.

The pedagogic relationship

Those of us whose professional lives are spent predominantly within tertiary education institutions can easily forget just how daunting the prospect of returning to education as a mature adult can be. The anxieties besetting many such individuals can serve to provoke a range of responses from a sort of paralysis, a tendency to over-react to events with extreme of emotion, and a consequent need for reassurance which many find hard to express. Despite having established and successfully managed their own companies with impressive turnovers and resulting profits the experiences of failure and rejection of school days from 20 or 30 years ago are all too evidently haunting many participants.

The sub-categories we identified under the heading of the pedagogic relationship were as follows:

- expectations that the relationship with facilitators will be 'real'
- reciprocity of learning between all those involved; participants, facilitators and sector specialists
- the benefits of interactive and participatory methods
- networking, either directly or indirectly
- awareness of progress, and
- reflection.

Establishing a sound working relationship with participants is an essential component in allaying fears, as is just being available, which can serve to dispel many early concerns, as Facilitator A outlines:

> "I mean, I certainly have much stronger relationships with my work-based students, just simply because I'm one-to-one with them regularly. So I would have no end of phone calls every day, emails and things ... weekends as well, where they will need to know something...It might be a basic question, it might be looking over a draft. So you have to be much more flexible with them."

It helps if the facilitator can relate to the culture of the workplace as Facilitator C notes:

> "I've found the process of adapting to 18-year-olds far more difficult than (to) work-based participants. Having been in industry myself, I found it very easy to adapt to working with work-based people, because I understood the need to be able to facilitate their learning from a standpoint of, 'I've come away from that and if we look back on it then ...'"

Facilitator B draws attention to the importance of peer support:

> "... they engage in a dialogue and they learn from each other. You can see that. And not the bad things as to how to avoid doing various things, or maybe plagiarising, but the good things. And the other thing, you know,(is) they inspire (each other), 'Can I see your draft?'"

Support and reassurance from facilitators and peers can create insights and breakthroughs for participants wrestling with problems, as Facilitator C observes:

> "... suddenly, somebody can sort somebody else's problem out because they're thinking in a different way and the person whose problem is solved thinks, 'Why didn't I think of that?' And that's basically because they were unable to step outside the box, because the box is all that they knew."

Reassurance also takes the form of providing regular and constructive feedback as Facilitator B points out:

> "...it (work-based learning) can be more challenging in a way because you give them sometimes two or three feedback(s) on two or three drafts, because they are very keen."

An adapted version of the Patchwork Text has been used on a number of programmes (See Dalrymple & Smith, 2008). The benefits of this approach to assessment are that it enables participants to complete short pieces of work early on in a programme, which can be turned around rapidly with constructive feedback thus allaying fears and providing advice on how to make improvements. Over an extended period we have found that it also provides a structured means of moving participants from a descriptive to a critical stance towards their studies, a topic which we will take up in Chapter 9.

Preparation in order to promote independent thinking is not quite everything, but it is an essential element in the active curriculum as Facilitator D suggests:

"I do purposely search out work case studies of the kind – "This was a scenario, what would you do in this case? ..." But part of the idea about bringing all these real work-based experiences is to give them a flavour of actually this is what the job role is really like and this is what it will entail, so that they know that they're going in the right direction ... I do lots of stuff with case work, case notes ... doing things where they have to bring in their own perspective, looking at their own bias and challenging that themselves ..."

And just as interactivity is deemed to be an important element of the work-based learning experience, so too is the more passive process of reflection as described by respectively by Facilitator C:

"So it's getting them to see and reflect on that link up between practice and theory, because if they don't (make those links) then they will always be an operational person ... therefore, they're moving in and out, tactical – operational, the whole time that they're there and it's that movement that creates the reflection, the thinking, and the ideas."

Facilitator B provides an example of how reflection enabled one participant on a work-based learning programme to make a significant transition in his learning and development:

*"(One participant had) been through the workshops, contributed some good points and was often a bit of a joker. In the final evaluation wash-up I said to them 'OK you've got five minutes to sort out what you've made of this programme and then you can feed it back to me.' Typical of these guys (military) the feedback was specific and without frills – really useful. Anyway he chimes in and says 'At first I thought this was a bit of ******* fluffy stuff, not for me, but then I started to think – I started to hear what I was saying and what the others were saying, and then I thought – 'This is OK, this is what I need.'"*

Implications for the curriculum

Much is made in the adult learning literature of the need for active, participatory methods (Knowles et al, 2011) and this is an emphasis with which we would concur. Designing and implementing such an approach is demanding as Facilitator A observes:

> *"So everything has to be tailor-made ... the materials, workshops themselves, everything. The purpose of those far more than anything is not really to do any kind of formal teaching. It's easier to get the group together and to get them talking about whatever research they want to be doing and to get to know each other and kind of gel as a cohort a little bit. Formal teaching ... it's difficult in that environment."*

As a consequence of the blurring of roles it is not unknown for peers to assume an interventional role on behalf of the facilitator as Facilitator D relates:

> *"But actually what happens in the end is I don't need to do so much challenging. Others learned to do it, very gently with this young lady and would say, 'Well, there's another point of view. Have you thought about this? What about – Do you think it might ...?' Those kinds of challenges."*

We have emphasised throughout this book the need for an integrated notion of curriculum to underpin effective work-based learning, indicating that each curricular element is in an organic relationship with the other elements, constituting a process of Learning in the Round. Sadly, systems of validation and accreditation, designed to satisfy the requirements of quality audit, tend to fragment programmes, often dramatically disaggregating the respective curricular elements. One of the consequences of this can be to confuse and distance all the actors from the central purposes of learning and development.

Teaching, learning and assessment methods need to be integrated, not aligned in a linear and uni-directional manner, but in an interactive and cyclical manner. This is particularly the case with regard to the processes of assessment and evaluation. Just as we are at pains to ensure that participants receive speedy and constructive feedback on drafts and assignments, we have become increasingly aware of the need to thread a range of evaluative approaches throughout workshops, ranging from the formal to the informal and the formative to the summative. The metaphor of assessment as a window into learning has been referred to for many years: just as the facilitator can gain insights into the participant's learning, so may the participants looking through the same window from the other side, gain insights into the facilitator's intentions and purposes. Learning in the Round seeks to provide as many windows as possible.

Conclusion

A consideration of the issues and approaches adopted by facilitators for work-based students in contrast to those of the traditional full-time students is productive. In some respects the 'gap' between the two groups has been eroded. Many full-time students engage in paid work for significant amounts of the week. Whereas this often involves quite restricted work roles, nonetheless the notion of having a student population disconnected from the day to day demands of the workplace is in most institutions increasingly a thing of the past.

Some of the tensions indicated in this chapter have therefore become issues in the lives of those regarded as traditional students; for example the challenges presented in managing conflicting demands and agendas. The need for a student to weigh the demands of the workplace against their own study needs is an experience common to both groups of learners.

Clearly, however, the contexts in which some of these work-based learners are operating offer a degree of challenge which is an order of magnitude beyond that which our 'traditional' students might face. Additionally, the developing careers of the work-based learners highlight the unavoidable tensions between study and the workplace demands which can become quite pronounced. This can be seen as a context informing the felt need amongst work-based students for immediacy of application. The idea that work-based participants seek 'real' relationships with facilitators is therefore not surprising. The demands of balancing the time commitment to learning alongside the achievement of organisational objectives are significant, requiring open and honest interchange and a shared recognition that all parties are Learning in the Round.

Postscript

At the time of revising this chapter one of the authors was completing a demanding schedule of interactive workshops with arena and event managers, social services personnel, and local authority middle managers. These experiences prompted a range of reflections on the challenges presented by the Learning in the Round approach, not least:

- when to intervene and
- to what extent to intervene
- judging the balance appropriately between presentation and active exploration by participants in view of the intended learning outcomes
- stepping back to allow specialists to mediate and interpret
- avoiding the teacher dangers of defaulting to the transmission mode – "I've prepared all this stuff, so you're going to get it." The facilitators have to reconcile themselves to the fact that they will prepare and have available far more material than they will use
- that the implications arising from this latter point suggest a bewildering range of issues regarding coverage and quality assurance which are worthy of further exploration.

Facilitating the process of Learning in the Round can be rewarding and stimulating; it can also be challenging and occasionally startling – standing outside the comfort zone can be chilling and it's as well for us to be reminded of that. It's what we ask the participants to do every day.

References

Dalrymple, R. & Smith, P. 2008. 'The Patchwork text: enabling discursive writing and reflective practice on a foundation degree in work-based learning.' *Innovations in Education & Teaching International. 45 (1). 47 – 54.*

Hoyle, E. (1976). The creativity of the school in Britain. In Harris et al (1975) (eds) Curriculum Innovation. London. Croom Helm in association with The Open University Press.

Knowles, M., Swanson, R. and Holton, E. (2011) The Adult Learner: A Neglected Species. 7th edn. London. Butterworth-Heinemann.

Trigwell, K. Martin, E. Benjamin, J. & Prosser, M. (2000). Scholarship of Teaching: a model. *Higher Education Research & Development. 19 (2). 155 – 168.*

Chapter Eight

Co-constructing the curriculum –
Learning in the Round in action

Gordon Vincent

A case study illustrating how a long-standing partnership between a local authority and a higher education institution (HEI) was able to realise the Learning in the Round process in the design and delivery of a range of professional development programmes. Charting the development of a foundation degree in working with children and young people; a short course in multi-disciplinary team working; a programme on applied commissioning; and a leadership programme for social work managers, the chapter identifies a continuum of provision in work-based learning that moves from universal professional development that is pre-specified by an HEI, through bespoke provision, to provision that is genuinely 'co-constructed' by the delivery partners – and indeed the participants.

Introduction

This chapter will offer a sustained example of the Learning in the Round process. It will relate how over a five-year period the children's services in a medium-sized shire Local Authority generated several substantial work-based programmes in professional development for staff working in education, social services, children's centres, Early Years and the voluntary sector. These programmes were derived from collaboration between participants, university-based facilitators and profession-based specialists and built on an interactive relationship between theoretical and practical knowledge, their focus firmly on the exploration and application of the resulting 'new knowledge' in the workplace. The chapter explains why this customised approach to workforce development was adopted, sets out the key features of each programme, and details how the process was refined over time until it came to approximate the Learning in the Round process espoused in this book. Reflection on the process reaffirms the value of postulating a dynamic model of work-based learning such as Learning in the Round.

Context of the programmes

The context for these four programmes, a foundation degree in working with children and young people; a short course in multi-disciplinary team working; a programme on applied commissioning; and a leadership programme for social work managers, was the promotion of integrated children's services through legislation and regulation, epitomised in the Children Act of 2004. This political initiative was driven, initially, by nationally imposed targets and central government funding. The chosen vehicle for delivery was local authorities which already served the whole child population and were answerable to locally elected members. However, the concept of a children's service also embraced all other agencies that worked with children and young people, including the voluntary and health services, the latter itself undergoing major re-organisation. The children's workforce was defined as all adults working full- or part-time with children and young people.

The legislation required each local authority to establish a Children's Trust, to co-ordinate the contributions of the different partners, and to appoint a director of children's services along with a workforce strategy lead. In this shire Authority these two posts were internal appointments and the new integrated children's service consisted largely of Council employees. So, with a few exceptions, the majority of the workforce in the new children's services in this local authority may have had a change of responsibilities and line-management, but in terms of conditions of employment and working practices, for many the change appeared not to be substantial. Nevertheless, the paradigm had changed: services were now to be focussed exclusively on the needs of the child or young person, utilising the expertise of other agencies, and achieving outcomes that improved children's life-chances.

Reculturing

Thus as in many situations where organisational development is required, there had been a reorganisation of personnel and functions; now the new organisation needed to 're-culture' (Fullan, 2001), a process informed in this instance by key players' prior experience of fostering collaborative leadership with schools (Durrant, 2007). By 2008, the government had made explicit the 'need to ensure that the children's workforce unites around a common purpose, language and identity' because 'integrated working is pivotal to a personalised service that responds to individuals' needs in a seamless and timely manner'. 'Strong, effective and supportive leadership and management at all levels within the system' was required with staff 'able to work comfortably in inter-agency and multi-disciplinary teams' (DCFS, 2008). Clearly, a suite of professional development programmes was required to face into this challenge.

Reculturing is a learning process: it involves nothing less than changing the culture of the organisation (Senge, 1990). The learning may be formal or informal, structured or unstructured, facilitated or self-directed, but it has a clear purpose and explicit outcomes. If successful, the learning is internalised and then evidenced in changes to attitudes, perceptions and practices in the workplace. The adult is motivated to learn by working with real concerns, solving real problems, and experiencing tangible improvements in performance. So, in this Authority, the emphasis was on creating reflective learning programmes that were targeted, participatory and experiential.

Partnering

Structural changes to organisations, such as co-locating multi-agency teams in children's centre, do not inevitably challenge values, demand new skills or change practice. Similarly, work-based learning can perpetuate poor practice if there is no external 'critical friend' to guide reflection and exploration of new knowledge. Likewise, it is important that the workforce perceives itself as a learning community with a strong moral imperative; in this case, meeting the needs of the child or young person. A close working partnership with a local university was thus sought to help create an active and inquiring learning community, the university partner providing the essential 'critical friendship' that helped avoid complacency or parochialism. Leaders were challenged, individuals were challenged; an organisational climate was created in which colleagues spoke of 'being on a journey', 'learning from each other' and 'being at the leading edge' -the latter perception being subsequently validated by Grade 1 OfSted inspection outcomes.

Curriculum philosophy

Boud and Solomon (2001) famously identified work-based learning as having the five key characteristics of negotiated learning plans; a focus on the needs of the workplace and the learner/employee; the prefacing of accreditation decisions with identifying learning needs; workplace learning tasks reflecting the needs of both the individual and the organisation; and the assessment of learning outcomes against external criteria. All of these elements were indeed attested in the educational philosophy shared by the partnership in the design and delivery of the programmes developed to meet this organisational development challenge. Early in the process however, it was felt that a flexible and dynamic model of work-based learning would best reflect the learning achieved on the programmes, not least because of the means by which core content and learning and teaching strategies were framed collaboratively; the curriculum was co-constructed.

This process of co-construction represented a departure for the local authority. Hitherto, when working with an HEI, the model of professional development employed in the county's children's services had involved the purchase of external professional development in 'off the peg' formats which, while they allowed a certain amount of tailoring of programme content, form and focus to specific participant needs, were nevertheless largely prescribed *in advance* by the higher education institution. In contrast, the three programmes developed in response to this specific organisational challenge were co-constructed from the outset by university academic staff and local authority colleagues working in partnership. Likewise, employers played a crucial role in creating and supporting the learning culture in which this transaction was encouraged and supported.

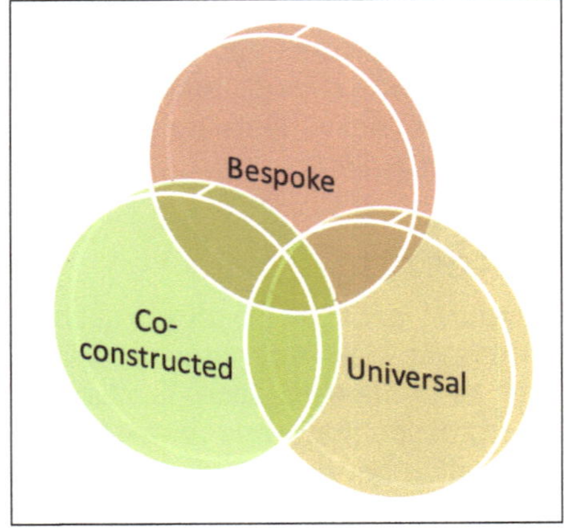

Figure One

It can be helpful to represent this continuum of increasingly participative modes of provision diagrammatically as shown in Figure One and described in the table below.

Universal provision	Bespoke provision	Co-constructed provision
Provision determined by an academic institution.	Components of universal provision selected through negotiation with employer.	Learning programme legitimated jointly by the academic institution and employees in the client group.
Generic knowledge illustrated by exemplars relevant to work-place.	Learning facilitated by managers in the academic institution and the workplace.	Employees engaged in the design, delivery and assessment of work-based collaborative learning.

With this continuum of provision held in mind, let us turn to look more closely at the detail of each of the three programmes and their proposed contribution to organisational and individual learning. While the programmes considered below were developed at different stages on this continuum from pre-specified provision, through bespoke provision to fully co-created provision, they all have a number of features in common. All programmes were underpinned by a shared ethical and pedagogic philosophy: first there is a clear and explicit moral imperative that children should have improved life-chances; second, there is an acceptance that collaboration is the norm and leads to better outcomes; third, there is a recognition that the needs of the child are often complex and require a multi-agency approach; fourth, there is agreement that good multi-agency leadership is difficult and needs training; fifth, there is an expectation that the workforce will contribute to the design and delivery of its own professional development; sixth, there is an external partner who is able to challenge parochialism and standards; and seventh, there is a value placed on the collective wisdom gained through the shared learning that brings together theory and practice.

Programme One: Multi-Agency Working

The first work-based Continuing Professional Development programme to be developed by this partnership was a short, Master's level course in multi-agency working, designed specifically to improve staff confidence and self-efficacy in working in multi-disciplinary teams. Historically, the professions serving the needs of children had long been separate and hierarchical institutions with collaboration at the margins of their practice. Thus a major challenge for an integrated children's workforce is to achieve more effective multi-agency working that better meets the complex needs of the child whilst retaining the benefits of specialist expertise. Accordingly, over a nine-month period, a programme was developed jointly by a team of staff drawn from across the different professions and the partner university that resulted in a two-year Foundation Degree in Working with Children and Young People which continues to enable non-graduates from different occupational areas to progress in the profession of their choice.

Programme Two: Leadership in Multi-Agency Settings

The second work-based programme was designed to address the need for improved leadership in children services. In line with the other changes and revisions being introduced, notions of leadership in the sector were being revisited and reconceptualised, with a particular emphasis on distributed and transformational leadership (Gill, 2011). No longer were managers able to rely on positional authority as in a hierarchical structure. Increasingly, at all levels, managers were expected to work laterally with colleagues whose authority, area of expertise, ethical codes, accepted practice, skill sets, access to resources and conditions of employment varied. In particular, they were required increasingly to give direction, engender 'followership', take risks and be held accountable. Change was both implicit and explicit in the new culture and needed to be led.

Thus, the same local authority/university partnership now co-developed a Diploma in Leadership in Multi-agency Settings where iterations of translating theory into practice became a cyclical process during a six-month multi-agency programme. Much of the 'new knowledge' was created through work-based assignments and reflection on experiences in the workplace. Access to this programme was increased by offering it at both undergraduate and postgraduate levels to allow for the different professional career routes. In line with its focus, the programme drew together markedly disparate participants in each cohort including staff working in safeguarding, children's centres, extended services, local delivery, primary and special schools, Early Years, Connexions, commissioning, and the voluntary sector.

As the number of staff benefiting from these programmes increased so the evidence of their effectiveness grew. Positive formal evaluations and recommendations from participants led to directors requesting other customised programmes for key sections of the workforce. This created the opportunity for participants, facilitators and sector specialists to work together even more closely, co-constructing a programme that met more precisely defined needs.

Programme Three: Applied Commissioning

The first of these new work-based programmes was designed for two-dozen commissioners who had recently been recruited and varied significantly in their experience and understanding of the role. The emphasis of the twelve-month in-house course was on 'applied' commissioning and the establishment of greater coherence and uniformity of practice across a large team. As well as the joint planning of content with the partner university, the participants agreed to tutor lunchtime seminars that became a core part of the accredited programme. Both the seminars and the main assignments reflected current issues identified by the team or addressed areas where practice could be further improved.

Programme Four: Leadership for Social Work Managers

The last of the four programmes, and that which was perhaps most customised to the specific context, invited over thirty social work managers to identify the needs of the individual, the team and their service in the light of a recent substantial report on safeguarding children (Munro, 2011). The result was an accredited leadership programme that offers participants the opportunity to explore, contextualise and model new ways of working.

Of course, whilst collaborative work-based learning with a higher education institution can assist in promoting a change of culture in an organisation, it need not take the form of accredited courses to be effective. The same shire Authority has also established regular multi-agency seminars for senior managers and elected members that challenge current thinking and practice. These have been structured to enable the underlying research to be presented by a university tutor with specialist expertise in the area followed by an outstanding practitioner. Each seminar concludes with a challenge to participants to identify and articulate the implications for their practice in front of colleagues. Recent topics have included the leadership of 'wicked problems' (Conklin, 2005); brain development and the use of evidence in early intervention (Allen, 2011); and securing public value through collaborative leadership (Grint & Brookes, 2010). Most of these themes have been further developed in one or more parts of the organisation. So, for example, commissioners are applying the principles of Social Value (SROI, 2012); there is now an aspiration that all staff and volunteers engaged in working with young children should have at least a Level 3 qualification that includes knowledge of brain development; and a Families First approach to intervention and support is being introduced.

Conclusions

This case study has sought to illustrate how curricular collaboration between a university and an organisation led to a progressively inter-dependent and synergistic relationship. Over the course of designing and delivering the four programmes explored above, an increasingly dynamic and flexible learning model was realised, congruent with the notion of Learning in the Round proposed in this book.

Such a process of co-construction not only sits well with the attested features of effective adult learning, involving an orientation to study that promotes autonomy and responsibility; the application of prior experience; and a practical dimension that motivates learning (Glaser, 2002; Murphy, 2002). In addition, the process provides for engagement in the learning process by the full range of stakeholders and maximises the opportunities for individual learning to be translated into wider organisational learning.

Mutual trust and respect between the academic institution and the employer would seem an obvious pre-requisite for effective co-construction of this kind but there also needs to be trust between the employee and employer that the learning programme agreed will be worthwhile and of value with a concrete application to the workplace. This trust has to be sustained throughout and can be severely challenged, even in a well-designed programme, if the quality of the provision does not meet the expectations of the learners. There needs to be a mechanism in the management of any co-constructed programme for issues to be identified and addressed quickly so that they do not diminish the motivation of the learners.

Finally, whilst the suite of programmes discussed in this case study remain current and relevant it is of course the case that a change of government and a revised policy context have already brought further changes for the sector in question. It is a further measure of the effectiveness of these programmes, and of the Learning in the Round process, that programme graduates are well placed to negotiate contexts of change and uncertainty, having acquired those skills of transferability and adaptability that are the signature of work-based learning at its most effective.

References

Boud, D. and Solomon, N. (2001). Work-based Learning. London. Oxford University Press/McGraw-Hill.

Conklin, J. (2005). Chapter 1: Wicked Problems and Social Complexity. In: Conklin J. Dialogue Mapping: Building Shared Understanding of Wicked Problems. London. Wiley

Durrant, J. (2007). By Us and For Us: Building Capacity for School Improvement through Collaborative Leadership and Professional Development – a study of four linked initiatives in Buckinghamshire. International Congress for School Effectiveness and Improvement. Slovenija, January. Canterbury Christ Church University.

England & Wales. Department for Children, Schools and Families (2008). 2020 Children and Young People's Workforce Strategy. London. DCSF Publications.

England & Wales. Department for Education (2011). The Munro Review of Child Protection: Final Report – A Child-centred System. London. HMSO.

England & Wales. Cabinet Office (2011). Early Intervention: the next steps. London. HMSO.

1. Office for Standards in Education, Children's Services and Skills

Fullan, M. (2001). Leading in a Culture of Change. San Francisco. Jossey-Bass.

Gill, R. (2011) (2nd ed). Theory and Practice of Leadership. London. Sage.

Glaser, R. (2002). Designing and Facilitating Adult Learning. HRDQ

Grint ,K.. & Brookes, S. (2010). Chapter 1, A New Public Leadership Challenge? In: Grint, K.. & Brookes, S. (eds). The Public Leadership Challenge. Basingstoke. Palgrave Macmillan,

Murphy, R. (2002). Facilitating Effective Professional Development and Change in Subject Leaders. NCSL.

Senge, P. (1990). The Fifth Discipline: The Art and Practice of the Learning Organisation. New York: Doubleday.

Chapter Nine
Getting critical: converting experience into understanding

Patrick Smith

A perennial issue with learners of all ages is helping them to manage the transition from thinking and writing descriptively, to thinking and writing with critical awareness. By the term critical awareness we mean the ability to exercise reason and judgement regarding the merits of something, along with the ability to present the results of these processes in ways which communicate effectively to others. Critical thinking involves a number of processes, such as the cognitive skills of recollection, interpretation, analysis, synthesis and judgement; however it also involves what might best be termed dispositions such as reflection and the determination

to go beyond what is evident, to surface and examine assumptions and values. In a refreshingly clear and practical discussion of aspects of critical reflection Facione (2011) defines critical thinking as:

> *"The process of purposeful, self-regulatory judgment, which uses reasoned consideration to evidence, context, conceptualizations, methods, and criteria."*

Facione is at pains to emphasise the importance of rooting considerations of critical thinking into the lives of learners as opposed to smothering them with abstract definitions of the concept. Such definitions tend to be remote and alien to learners and therefore of little use to them. This approach is very much in line with our position of starting at the point which the participant occupies.

In Chapter Three we referred to the importance of enabling participants to realise that theory is not a remote, academic concept, but an everyday stance towards the world governing what we do and why we do it. Part of the facilitator's role is to help participants access and realise those theories in terms of beliefs, assumption and consequent actions and to articulate them amongst their peers in order to subject them to scrutiny and discussion within classrooms and workshops. Once the realisation comes that there are few, if any, single and absolute solutions and that actions are conditioned by circumstances, then participants can move on to refine and develop their understandings in order to focus them in pursuit of solutions to fresh problems, applying and adapting their understandings as they proceed.

In practical terms facilitating these transitions involves shifting from personal 'worlds' into the 'worlds' of those others; it means crossing boundaries of both understanding and behaviour, and of entering into foreign settings where differences stand out in sharp contrast. Miscommunications and misunderstandings which can be resolved with relative ease in face-to-face settings can assume far greater significance in classrooms where the development of understanding, knowledge and skills are the principal intentions. Add to this mix the additional element of that power inherent in the traditional role of the teacher and the potential for misunderstanding and not learning is amplified.

We suggest that communication between the respective actors involved – participant, specialist and facilitator – is crucial. This chapter seeks to explore aspects of communication in the classroom and workshop by looking at some features of academic culture which can seem unrelated and alien to mature and experienced individuals. It then goes on to outline a practical means – in this case a Pyramid Exercise – of rooting learning in the world of the participant in order to develop within them those elements of critical enquiry which are the hallmark of a higher education.

When cultures collide

The language of the academic and the understandings, practices and assumptions that it embodies, can be in sharp contrast to that of the participant. Each views the communication register of the other with a degree of scepticism and suspicion. I suggest that the greater the divide, the greater the chances for mutual non-communication, disappointment and failure. This difference in cultures can be more exaggerated and damaging when the participant is a mature and experienced adult whose previous experience of education was 15 or 20 years ago.

The world that the participant inhabits in the workplace is characterised by its familiarity and its immediacy in terms of need, application, practicality and problem solving. In contrast the world the participant enters can appear remote, theoretical and concerned with creating problems where no problems appear to exist. It can appear to be a different and thoroughly alien environment. The cultures of the world of work and the world of the university stand in stark contrast, as Graff illustrates:

"As teachers we often proceed as if the rationale of our most basic academic practices is understood by our students, even when we get plenty of signs to the contrary. We take for granted, for example, that reflecting in a self-conscious way about experience – 'intellectualising' – is something that students naturally see the point of and want to learn to do better."
(Graff, 2002)

Graff goes on to identify three counter-intuitive academic practices that further emphasise the cultural divide. The first is that of making problems out of that which does not seem problematic to participants:

"Nothing better exemplifies the apparently counter-intuitive nature of intellectual practices than their [academics] obsession with what appear to be bogus 'problems.'"
(ibid)

He then notes that a fairly natural and normal participant response might well be:

'Why go looking for problems? They occur often enough without looking for them.'
(ibid)

The second and third seemingly counter-intuitive practices are related and are concerned with argument and counter argument, in short with adopting positions which are in opposition. The process of arguing a point and of adopting a counter position can appear to be unnecessarily confrontational, aggressive and uncomfortable unless the reasons of testing the strength of a position along with the nature and quality of the evidence supporting it are made clear.

These practices, implicitly embedded in academic practice, are unfamiliar to participants, whilst the practice of the posing of issues in dualistic and dichotomous terms is not only both negative and restricting, (Shulman, 1988), but can further emphasise the gap between the incoming participant and the university.

What are we doing here?

It might be well to consider at this stage why we are all in Room G2.17 on a wet Monday afternoon in November when the heating does not appear to be working and estates has chosen this time to replace the insulation in the ceiling voids all around G2.17. Allegedly we are concerned with education whose function is about instruction and the creation of understanding, and whose origins lie in notions of 'leading out.'

One of the principal functions of the facilitator in leading out participants, I would suggest, is to bridge the gap between themselves and the learners, in order to engage those participants in their own learning and to make new and different ideas accessible to them. Northedge (2003) refers to teachers taking participants on 'excursions' in order to enable them to engage them progressively in the processes of academic discourse.

Mature adults represent huge reservoirs of knowledge and experience, resources which not only have the potential to enrich and inform the learning of themselves and their peers, but also enable them to appreciate the reasons for and the benefits of theory, reflection, analysis and the development of a critical stance. It would seem prudent therefore to emphasise that these common academic notions of theory, critical analysis, synthesis and the making of reasoned, logical judgements are appreciated by participants. After all these are the tools in the academic toolbox and it were better that they were made understandable and familiar to the participants, rather than having participants remain ignorant of the purposes of these tools. We are in the business of developing informed and well-rounded participants, so it must follow that we would want them to be equipped with a toolbox, or repertoire of learning skills, rather than just a single skill, if only on the basis that a person with hammer is in danger of seeing every problem as a nail.

Having discussed some general differences in terms of cultures between the world of academia and the workplace, the next section will consider four specific and related concepts, those of being critical, the role of theory and notions of analysis and synthesis.

Being critical

I have already suggested that language is tricky, that a common term may have a range of different meanings. This is the case with the concept of being critical, which has two principal meanings. The first is that of disapproval of a person, thing or idea based on perceived errors, short-comings or faults, whilst the second is concerned with a judgement based on the analysis of the relative merits or faults of an artefact or piece of work. Broadly speaking the first definition is more commonly used in society, whilst the second is what the university tutor is seeking in the outputs of his/her participants. In short, critical is not bad and destructive; it seeks to develop more precise understandings, to be discriminate and to provide coherent and logical reasons for understandings and actions. Critical analysis – that term beloved of writers of intended learning outcomes – as stated at the beginning of this chapter, is concerned with that process by which a participant demonstrates comprehension of ideas and compares the respective merits of these ideas against explicit standards or criteria of judgement. In short, it is my opinion that this is so because of X, Y and Z and I make this judgement against the standards of A, B and C. You may not agree with me and that is then the basis for us to discuss, to argue even.

The role of theory

The notion of theory is one which also suffers from a range of interpretations and assumptions which bear little scrutiny. "Oh, that's alright in theory…"

we respond when what someone is saying appears to have little relevance or practical use. "…it's airy fairy theory" suggesting that it is little more than whimsy, something insubstantial, like smoke in the air or steam rising from the road after rain, something and nothing.

It seems to me that there are two aspects of theoretical understandings which are crucial to learning. First that each of us operates on theories, whether we know it or not, and second that, as Lewin (2001) puts it, there is nothing as practical as a good theory.

The first suggestion is that we all work from theories. The term theory I take to refer to a set of understandings and beliefs which are intended to explain something, an idea, a technique and/or a system of beliefs and ideas. These understandings and beliefs are based on general and explicit principles, which are independent of that which is being explained. Whether we are driving a bus, building a wall, attempting to negotiate the intricacies of internet banking, or trying to unravel notions of time and space in relation to the galaxy, we are all referring, either consciously or unconsciously, to beliefs, assumptions and understandings about the nature of that with which we are concerned. We are all working from a theory, be it implicit, tacit and private or explicit, vocal and public. To be aware of the theory we are working from is to be able to consider its practicality and effectiveness in a given set of circumstances and furthermore to be in a position to develop that theory in order to make it more effective. Thus one of the roles of the facilitator inevitably must be to help the participant to become aware of their own theories, to evaluate their usefulness and to entertain new and alternative theories. This is the notion of metacognition – arguably a crucial skill that a participant can develop – a notion to which we return below.

The second point above follows from this, which is that the more informed and discriminating the participant can become in the selection and use of theoretical understandings and approaches, the more effective their practice becomes. Or to put it another way, the more tools one has available, along with the knowledge of how to use them, the more effective can be the outcomes of their use. Hence, nothing is more practical than a good theory.

Metacognition

We have referred throughout this book to the importance of all three actors developing their reflective and metacognitive capabilities. Whilst the definition of the concept of metacognition remains 'elusive' (Gamache, 2002), with no universally agreed definition, we take it to refer to the ability to monitor the effectiveness of one's actions and strategies in order to evaluate their effectiveness and to make changes 'on the hoof' in order better to pursue a given agenda and/or objective, or respond to emerging issues, questions or related topics. The facilitator in the Learning in the Round setting has to possess a broad 'corridor of tolerance' (McAlpine et al, 1999) enabling them to stand aside from what is happening in order to assess it.

The advantages of all the actors developing effective self-evaluating strategies is acknowledged as a significant determinant of professional learning, (Eraut, 2009; Jackson, 2004). For both Boud & Soloman (2000) and Raelin (2008) metacognition is central to work-based learning. The benefits of learners developing as self-directed learners, capable of organising, implementing and evaluating their learning strategies are set out by Bolhuis & Voeten (2004) in their depiction of self-directed learning.

Analysis and synthesis

Much is made of the twin concepts of analysis and synthesis as generic tools in the educational toolbox and rightly so. It is important that participants perceive both their significance and utility.

Analysis is concerned with the identification of the constituent elements of an artefact, concept or communication, the relationships between those parts and the ways in which they are organised. Essentially it is concerned with breaking down and mapping that item. It involves distinguishing between fact and supposition, and between that which is significant and that which is extraneous.

By contrast synthesis involves the assembling of separate elements in order to create a whole, be it an artefact, concept or communication. In writing this chapter I am attempting to synthesise my ideas about how experience can be converted into knowledge and understanding on the part of participants. To synthesise then is:

> *"...a process of working with elements, parts, etc., and combining them in such a way as to constitute a pattern or structure not clearly there before."*
> *(Bloom et al, 1956: 162)*

In order to get participants to translate their experience into explicit knowledge and understanding then, analysis and synthesis are essential elements.

In what follows I will outline an approach intended to relate personal and private experience through critical analysis into explicit and public understanding – in short, to convert experience into understanding.

The Pyramid Exercise

Thus far I have suggested that experienced adults undertaking university programmes of study can be faced with challenges in the form of culture shocks, and that tutors are in a position to facilitate the transition from workplace to university in order to optimise the positive outcomes for those concerned. I have also presented and explored concepts which represent the everyday tools of the academic, which participants are expected to understand and manage.

In this section I will outline an approach which seeks to facilitate the participant's transition from thinking and writing descriptively about their own experiences and understandings, to thinking and writing critically by means of discussion and group work.

The Pyramid Exercise is something of a hardy perennial in the facilitation of participant learning. Its principal virtues are that it is flexible, requires participants to engage and with deft structuring on the part of the tutor can be used to pass control over to the participants and bring it back when the intentions have been achieved. It is also a means of getting the participants to develop a basic conceptual map of an area of study, which can subsequently be referred back to in order to relate to concepts and to consolidate learning.

The operation of the Pyramid Exercise is summarised in Figure One below. For the purposes of illustration we will refer to two ways in which the pyramid can be used; the first focuses on how people learn and the second is concerned with introducing basic notions of leadership and management. In the interests of brevity and space we will sketch in general points as indicators.

Figure One. The Pyramid Exercise.

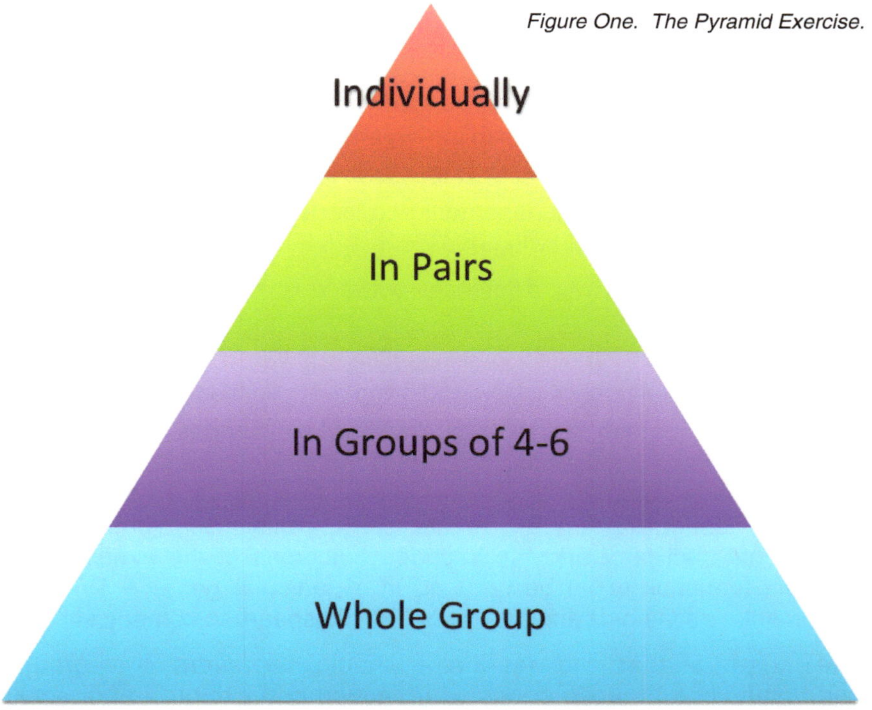

For the purposes of illustration we will focus on two areas, those of learning and management and leadership.

In the Pyramid Exercise participants are required individually to prepare a brief descriptive outline from their own experiences as a learner, or of being led or managed. The emphasis here is on the recall of an actual event or events and their description of that event. This usually takes 7 – 10 minutes and participants are asked to complete it in silence, (though it is remarkable how often their minds go blank when asked to recall their experiences!). If individuals are completely stumped then I will often allow them to move to the next stage.

The second stage involves working in pairs. Each presents their accounts to the other. The purposes here are concerned with clarification, the provision of examples if necessary and the expansion of any significant points. At this stage discussions tend to be descriptive, though significant and influential factors might well be referred to. This stage of the exercise takes between 10 and 15 minutes.

The third stage occurs in groups of four to six people. The participants are required to re-present their accounts and to respond to three or four prompt questions which start the process of identifying significant factors. Typically groups will be allowed 30+ minutes in which to complete this stage of the exercise, record their findings and to prepare short feedback presentations.

In relation to the process of learning the prompt questions might be:

- Can you identify different ways of learning?
- What factors are common to the experiences of the group?
- What role did teachers play in the learning?

In relation to notions of management and leadership, the groups may be tasked to consider the following questions:

- Can you identify any differences between what managers do and what leaders do?
- Are there different types of managers and leaders?
- If there are differences, how would you describe them?

With the whole group reconvened the individual groups are tasked to feedback and present their findings. This feedback can be straightforward by means of a summary flipchart sheet, or Post-its, or it can be more elaborate, depending on the nature of the relationship between the participants, facilitator and the intended outcomes of the exercise. For example feedback might be required in a particular genre – TV Soap, Documentary style or dramatic style, ie: Shakespearean comedy etc.

The point is that the feedback should represent the groups' understandings of those concepts identified and explored and should be available for subsequent reference to serve as a conceptual map of the topic area. Typically in relation to learning and teaching central issues emerge, such as the role of motivation, the influence of good or bad teachers (sadly too often the latter predominate), the importance of tenacity, different preferences and styles of learning, and learning to learn. Whilst in relation to management and leadership notions of who is expected to do what might appear, different types of leader from the hero model to the transformational might be cited, along with issues such as delegation, communication and the benefits and perils of working in teams. The process will also have raised questions which the facilitator should record in order to address as the session moves on.

With the participants having created a general conceptual map of the field the facilitator is then in a position to begin to explore particular aspects of that field or topic referring back to the conceptual maps and introducing theory where appropriate to inform those observations presented in the conceptual maps. For example, in relation to learning, notions of learning preference and style can be explored further by reference to the range of inventories available, whilst both their utility and reliability can be assessed by reference to the work of Coffield et al (2004) – a recent and comprehensive review of the notion of learning styles and those inventories which purport to measure it.

In relation to management and leadership distinctions between the two concepts can be explored by reference to, for example, Zaleznik (1992), whose discussion of the essential differences between the two concepts remains an influential, though potentially confusing, work, since it raises the broader issue of there being different perspectives on common phenomena – a useful lesson for the novice to grasp.

The conceptual maps developed by the participants will not cover the entire field of study, but there will be successive opportunities for the facilitator to refer to what the groups have identified as distinctive and significant as s/he sets out to present and explore the field. In this way the experiences of individuals can be related through discussion with their peers and the facilitator to the broader realms of theory. It is not unusual for individuals to find this process by turns edifying, surprising and reassuring, as exemplified by reactions such as:

> *"That's what I've kind of done for years without knowing why – it makes sense now."*

To which the facilitator, ever ready to nail a learning point down, can respond with:

> *"Now you know why, you can see that you have a range of other approaches/ strategies that you could use, don't you?"*

The point is that the work which originated with the participants can be used in such a way as to provide springboards for the presentation and critical analysis of different theoretical positions, thus hopefully making theory relevant to and not distant from what participants understand and do in the workplace.

Discussion

We would not claim that this approach is exclusive, or that it always enjoys complete success, but it has a number of features which recommend it to both participants and facilitators. Experience suggests that time spent in thinking through what the facilitator wants the participants to do in terms of the prompt and tasking questions, is time well spent, and that time observing how the participants behave and react provides clues and cues to levels of comprehension and pointers to be picked up and dealt with subsequently. At any point however the facilitator might be required to exercise his/her metacognitive capabilities, to change tack, to track back or sideways in order to illustrate how an observation and/or insight developed by the participants relates to what is known theoretically, and vice-versa.

Experience also demonstrates that the following features of this approach are advantageous and worthy of consideration, since it:

- is socially-based
- allows the facilitator to pass control to the participants and to take it back when necessary
- relates lived experience to theoretical understandings and perspectives
- promotes discussion and dialogue between all those involved
- closes or even bridges the gap between workplace and academy
- often convinces the anxious and uncertain that their experiences and knowledge are worthwhile and valuable.

Perhaps the most significant lesson that participants can learn through this process is that of owning the learning process by means of relating lived and recollected experience to universal understandings of phenomena. The participant is not alone.

References

Bloom, B. Englehart, M. Furst, E. Hill, W. & Krathwohl, D. (1956). Taxonomy of educational objectives. London. Longmans.

Bolhuis, S. & Voeten, J. (2004). Teachers' conceptions of student and own learning. *Teachers & Teaching: Theory & Practice. 10 (1). 77 – 98.*

Boud, D. & Soloman, N. (2000). Working as the curriculum: pedagogical and identity implications. UTS Research Centre Vocational Education & Training Working Knowledge: productive learning at work. University of Technology, Sydney, New South Wales, Australia.

Coffield, F. Moseley, D. Hall, E & Ecclestone, K. (2004). Learning styles and pedagogy in post-16 learning. London. The Learning and Skills Research Centre.

Eraut, M. (2009). How professionals learn through work. http://learningtobeprofessional, pbworks.com/

Facione, P. (2011). Critical thinking: what it is and why it counts. Insightassessment.com

Gamache, P. (2002). University students as creators of personal knowledge: an alternative epistemological view. *Teaching in Higher Education. 7 (3). 277 – 294.*

Graff, G. (2002). The problem problem and other oddities of academic practice. *Arts & Humanities in Higher Education. 1 (1). 27 – 42.*

Jackson, N. (2004). Developing the concept of meta-learning. *Innovations in Education & Teaching International. 41 (4). 391 – 403.*

Lewin, K. (2001). http:www.infed.org/thinkers/et-lewin.htm

Northedge, A. (2003). Enabling participation in academic discourse. *Teaching in Higher Education. 8 (2). 169 – 180.*

Raelin, J. (2008). Work-based learning. San Francisco. Jossey-Bass.

Shulman, L. (1988). The dangers of dichotomous thinking. Chapter 2 in Grimmett & Shulman "Reflection in Teacher Education." New York. Teachers College & Columbia University.

Zaleznik, A. (1992). Managers and leaders: are they different? *Harvard Business Review. March – April.*

Chapter 9 Getting critical: converting experience into understanding

Chapter Ten
Emerging trends and issues

Patrick Smith, Chris Kemp, Teresa Moore
and Roger Dalrymple

Introduction

For many years now the only constant in education has been change and currently the landscape of tertiary education is altering fundamentally as we move into uncertain and uncharted territories. Changes abound, from free-market schooling initiatives, to calls from industry for bespoke and closed qualification programmes for singular or shared organisations. Such programmes provide education, training and the delivery of ever smaller bite-sized chunks of what can only be described as immediate highly focused provision for companies eager for knowledge rather than the qualifications that go with it. At the same time the commercial sector is demanding – and in increasing numbers originating its own – bespoke content and delivery, heralding a more corporate age for education.

With this in mind one wonders how the traditional education sector will survive in the long term. Fundamental changes are already occurring as represented by Derby University creating a corporate arm to deal with industry, clearly separated from its traditional academic arm. Such a move, whilst receiving adverse and hostile reactions from many educationists, represents a courageous and radical departure. It is pioneering a way forward which divides opinion in terms of what it represents in terms of implications for education and training – bad in the sense that it flies in the face of traditional beliefs which determine how knowledge is structured, delivered and assimilated; good in the sense that it exposes the sector's weaknesses. These weakness centre on the sector's inability to create an education for all and to allow that education to develop its own identity.

Delivering a diet of education and training that is fit for purpose is a key driver behind this book and the Learning in the Round concept is a mature way of approaching and managing the salient aspects of a hitherto piecemeal process.

It is worth repeating that the process outlined and promoted in this book is neither the finished product, nor was it achieved in the orderly way in which our account might appear to suggest. The account presented here is retrospective and in the interests of clarity, along with perhaps a touch or two of 20:20 hindsight, it is susceptible to distortion in the interests of trying to provide a coherent narrative. Like the progress of individual participants on the programmes on which accounts are based, progress has often been erratic – characterised by reversals, disjunctures, sudden breakthroughs and occasionally:

"... those delicious outcomes that constitute the surprises of educational experience."
(Eisner, 2000: 344)

As identified above such a process by definition is chancy, problematic, organic and evolving, with decisions about pedagogic form, content and approach often made expediently on the basis of what seemed appropriate at the time – in line with the 'creative, imaginative and flexible approaches' espoused by Moore and Workman (2011). However the decisions made were based on that set of values and assumptions which were established early on and which provided a foundation to what we do and why we do it that way – primary values and assumptions, such as:

- viewing learning as both a personal and social process as well as being ubiquitous, infectious and possibly viral
- the importance and value of what each actor potentially can contribute
- an openness and willingness to engage in dialogues which are creative stimulating and generative
- collaboration as a means of exploring experiences and ideas in order to create insight and understanding with which to inform future practice
- trust and mutual regard whilst acknowledging difference
- the power and value of reflection
- a willingness to 'take a punt' possibly to fail, to recognise and accommodate uncertainty and ambiguity
- the accommodation of conditions of constant change both semiotically and in terms of an appropriate format to meet the needs of the actors.

In the light of these latter characteristics, there is some comfort and reassurance to be drawn from Daniel Dennett's recent observation:

"Any being, any agent who can truly say 'Well, it seemed like a good idea at the time' is standing on the threshold of brilliance."
(Dennett, 2013)

We make no claims to brilliance, but we do aspire to it and hope that what we can make a claim to is practice which is authentic, pragmatic and transformative.

This final chapter presents and explores what we consider to be the significant emerging trends and issues in work-based higher education. The chapter will focus upon four salient themes:

- the importance of work-based learning in modelling the curriculum shift from generic to bespoke provision
- the role and implications of technology and social media in work-based learning programmes

- the scalability and transformative capacity of learning
- work-based learning: with or without the academy.

We are mindful that in seeking to anticipate future developments it is possible to start plausibly enough with concrete and recognisable elements, but their exploration can, like ideologically based argument, make sudden and subtle transitions as rational discussion is determined by implicit assumptions which take the form of articles of faith. It is our intention however to remain as firmly as possible with our feet on the ground; acknowledging that those assumptions which underpin our practice inevitably will colour and influence the form and content of our discussion.

Work-based learning and curriculum shift from generic to bespoke provision

A marked emerging trend attested in this book and in other studies in this field (Reeve and Gallagher, 2005; Felce, 2010) is the increasing importance of collaborative curriculum development in work-based learning and the likelihood that it will increasingly be adopted as a model for curriculum development more widely. The current sector-wide emphasis upon student experience; transferable skills or employability; and, increasingly, personalised learning pathways, means that work-based learning curricula have much to offer all sectors as examples of differentiated provision. As the case study related by Gordon Vincent in Chapter Eight demonstrates, co-production of the curriculum and tailoring of provision to specific learning needs is an increasingly familiar part of the work-based learning experience. This case study is representative of a much wider process of curriculum-making within those institutions that are actively engaged in work-based learning. Consequently, expertise is growing in moving from generic curricular provision to more tailored offerings – this tailoring extending well beyond the optionality of certain content long associated with traditional modular programmes and instead extending into the very form and focus of education programmes.

This change of conception can also extend to revising our thinking about qualifications and the curriculum. Whilst traditional 'in-house' curriculum design in institutions will tend to take as its starting point the target award (and perhaps some associated exit awards) that a student might select, the experience of work-based learning curriculum design is more fluid, with decisions as to the most appropriate qualification structure often being reached after the process of curriculum design. This represents a 'live' curriculum, organically responding to those factors at work in the context within which it is set – far from the generic prescriptions of much that currently passes for educational provision.

The shape of things to come: face-to-face and remote. If technology is the answer, then what is the question?

For those who have stayed with us in this book, it will come as no surprise that we set great store by those interactions and relationships that occur in classrooms and workshops – the 'touchy-feely' stuff. On the other hand however we are acutely aware of the increasingly influential role played by emerging communications and social media technologies in supporting and facilitating work-based learning (Niea et al, 2011). A particular interest of ours concerns achieving the optimum blend of face-to-face and remote contacts and communication.

Experience demonstrates that there is no single solution to achieving such a balance or blend. For all the emphasis that we place on face-to-face encounters, it is important to acknowledge the achievements over recent decades of the Open University whose direct contacts with students are minimal and whose guidance on work-based learning have informed the wider sector (Open University, 2006).

Whilst email represents a convenient means of communication, particularly of administrative details and arrangements, as a means of substantive communication it has clear limitations, not least those arising from the informality of expression which characterises many postings. Nevertheless as a means of 'pinging' first drafts as attachments and for indicating sources or references for subsequent follow-up, it is both efficient and reliable. Our experience of Virtual Learning Environments (VLEs) as a work-based learning tool is less positive. Used as repositories for resources the VLE has obvious attractions in terms of access; however the interactive elements such as Posting Boards and Forums rarely, in our experience, generate much traffic, though activity does tend to spike around assignment deadlines on those programmes with regular assessment points and participation can be boosted when such activities are synchronous (Dennen, 2005). However in the main tracking usage can be a dispiriting activity in the light of the time and effort invested in populating the VLE.

The emergence of Skype and teleconferencing platforms on the other hand has been a more positive experience both in respect of managing one-to-one and group communications. Apart from the minor inconveniences of crowding together in order to appear on screen in group communications, the advantages of being able to see reactions and non-verbal cues represents a significant contribution to effective communications, quite apart from the fact that to the non-expert it appears to be a relatively simple piece of technology working with apparent ease both within and across continents.

Massive Open Online Courses (MOOCs) represent the opening of educational provision for all, price, access and availability no longer presenting barriers to education. On the face of it MOOCs may seem to be the antithesis of work-based learning given their universality; however we suggest that they have the potential to exist in a symbiotic relationship which may well see the MOOC as an integral part of work-based learning repertoire of resources in the future.

What we are referring to here is the notion of Digital- and Trans-literacy which are only two of the many issues now being discussed as a result of the increasing use of digital technologies and platforms in learning and teaching. As the use of Twitter, Facebook and blogs increases the dissemination of materials and resources, stimulating communication, comment and information, questions are being raised about technological democracy and whether there is accessibility for all. The levels of digital and/or trans-literacy skills needed to participate, also raise questions about the levels of audience engagement, not just how many engage, but to what extent and at what level they engage. These in turn raise questions about the effectiveness and impact of social media, along with its use in teaching and learning. In short a complex set of evaluative issues is raised.[1]

Our experience with conference calls, in both audio and video formats, has been limited principally by compatibility issues. Whilst we have used audio conference calls, even running action learning sets with five members in a room and the sixth on the end of a phone, the natural flow of communication has been stilted, contributions being punctuated by pauses, two or more people then speaking at once and embarrassed silences. Video conferencing has the advantage of contributors being able to see and better 'read' each other, but again, as a function of the limitations of the technology, compatibility and the time spent in setting up has proved less than effective. Perhaps the problem here lies in the relative lack of sophistication of both the technology and facilitator expertise as users.[2] This can be a particular embarrassment when working with participants whose professional lives are spent communicating globally via a range of conferencing platforms – they are apt to roll their eyes upwards and shake their heads prior to commiserating with their facilitators.

Recently one of the authors conducted a transatlantic experiment as part of a three-phase festival consultancy in which initially the paperwork for the festival was scrutinised and analysed producing a Needs Analysis. This was followed up by a series of teleconferences. From this process a four-hour Webex training seminar was conducted following which a specialist

---

1   For an interesting and practical SEDA discussion of some of these issues see: www.http://davidbaume.com/handouts-for-seda-may-conference

2   The phenomenon of learner facility with technology outstripping that of their teachers is increasingly prevalent across sectors a topic which has been recently charted by a Higher Education Academy study by Jones & Shao (2011).

visited the festival to deliver consultancy on site. We suggest that this represents a paradigm example of blended learning, drawing on remote and face-to-face interactions mediated via appropriate technologies. This type of approach enables a more flexible working arrangement which can bring together a range of actors as well as making more economic use of time and resources.

Such initiatives and approaches represent our initial and tentative steps into exploring the possibilities of blended learning. Rather than pursue the route of seeking ever more sophisticated technologies, we have tended to retreat to the simple, the tried and relatively trusted. Our real concerns have been and remain how to reconcile the elements of face-to-face and remote interactions in order to establish an effective balance. In short to identify what the significant factors are and how they might be organised and managed in order to optimise learning. Technological advances would appear to offer new possibilities for association and the creation of virtual communities which are not only transitory, coalescing around issues of immediate interest and concern, but which are leaderless and potentially democratising – for good or ill.

Social media

As the ubiquity of social media becomes ever more apparent educators need both to understand and to adapt to new learning environments and the opportunities they represent. In a work-based learning context, we are beginning to learn how social media both facilitate and change the learning experience. Firstly by enabling learning to take place anywhere, anytime and through a variety of digital platforms, the relationship between the actors – facilitator, participant, specialist – is altered. In conditions where it is easier to access, to communicate and make almost immediate use of guidance, social media more than ever before could be said to be a perfect platform for supporting Learning in the Round.

Secondly we suggest an equal, arguably a more significant factor. By its very nature social media introduce an element of reportage into daily life which can be harnessed by the facilitator and integrated into the process of learning. This reportage aspect of social media engages the actors in a process of continual update, comment and reflection on current experiences and opinions. Furthermore it provides an opportunity for educators to develop reflective learning beyond the point where once, and it now seems almost artificially, the participant was encouraged or even tasked to write a reflective piece in the form of a log, journal or essay. Given these conditions, the creation of a reflective element running alongside learning and work-based experiences elevates that feature's significance and relevance to learning. No longer is it an external task, potentially an imposition to be undertaken, completed and submitted for appraisal. Now it is possible for this critical element to become an intrinsic element of learning, a natural concomitant of a way of life.

As educators we are really novices at the beginning of our own digital revolution and need better to understand how to develop and use the potential of social media in the learning process. We need to develop our understanding of how social media are changing the way that individuals engage with their experiences, be it at work, entertainment, or in personal relations, and then to learn how to harness that propensity for reflective comment in order to enhance the learning dynamic. Further consequences will undoubtedly centre around resourcing and the location of control, for he who pays the piper is likely to call the tune.

We would do well to remember that social media are not a universal panacea. Their use occasionally can and have caused significant damage, such as creating panic as a result of misinformation; a condition which can impact on work-based learning. As Tuan (1974) states:

> *"In modern society vision tends to be emphasised at the expense of other senses, as the others require proximity and slow-pace to function ... culture can influence perception to the degree that people will see things that do not exist: it can cause group hallucination."*
> *(Tuan, 1974: 6)*

Learning scope and scale: transformative learning

We take learning scope and scale to refer to the transformative consequences for participants, which manifests in their confidence not only to undertake Learning in the Round, but to include and capitalise upon the cumulative effects that successful learning has on the them and their ability to operate successfully within the work context. Given the conditions of a supportive environment, as we have seen exemplified in Chapters Five, Six and Seven, the participant is able to develop enhanced levels of confidence in their own capabilities in applying theory to practice as we saw with Participant A, "They didn't realise how much I knew." This very statement, it might be suggested, represents a realisation by Participant A herself of how much she knew, perhaps she had to articulate it in order to realise and apprehend fully its implications.

Work-based learning at its best, we argue, provides a platform for the participant to grow in confidence and gradually to assume control of his/her learning. In short it enables the learner to reconceptualise previous understandings as part of the transformation process as previously outlined in Chapter Two. One of many examples is that of Carl, an experienced special forces operative who at the final debrief of a series of workshops contributed his considered reflections:

"At first I thought it was a bunch of tree-huggers, but after the third or fourth workshop – we'd been looking at learning profiles, I think – there was like a light, something happened and I could see what you were getting at."

This Damascene moment would prove significant, launching Carl on a journey of self-directed study which currently finds him as a qualified Myers-Briggs instructor and with a master's qualification completed successfully.

This extension of learning scope and scale is not an unproblematic linear process, but one which is characterised by diversions and detours. Ultimately it is by means of this process that participants grow in confidence and come to believe that they can push their learning and practice to higher levels. Typically we have found that those who fully engage often go on to undertake higher level education qualifications with relish and enthusiasm, possibilities which would once have been daunting and disabling prospects, if considered at all.

Work-based learning beyond the walls: within or without the academy?

Given the gathering momentum and established benefits of work-based learning in education over the last twenty years, the question also begged is whether it will increasingly become normalised as a field of knowledge within established institutions, or whether it might take another form, removing itself almost entirely from institutional ties to assume an independent and autonomous existence focusing on identified workplace needs and drawing eclectically on expertise and resources as necessary.

Moves towards the former scenario can be seen in the increased willingness of a wider spectrum of education institutions to recognise experiential learning and to grant academic credit and entry with advanced standing to their programmes (Scott, 2010; Moore and Workman, 2011). It is possible to foresee a snowballing effect whereby the more tertiary education providers involve themselves in accrediting work-based learning, the more a set of norms is established for regarding work-based and experiential learning as commensurate with certain kinds of established academic learning – such as the knowledge embodied in the curricula of the practice disciplines of nursing and teaching (Hodge et al, 2011). It may well come about that the activity of 'work-based learning' becomes increasingly constituted allied to these practice disciplines with their established experience of placement learning and practice education. In that sense, whilst remaining generative of Gibbons's 'Mode 2 knowledge' (1994), work-based learning programmes might in time become more familiar with elements of the curriculum across the tertiary sector.

On the other hand, conditions are sufficiently uncertain and turbulent that work-based learning, which we have elsewhere described as 'academy aligned' (Dalrymple, Kemp and Smith, 2012), detaches from formal education. In short, work-based learning might return to its origins, being a blend of the incidental, the purposed and the informal. This time however it has the advantage of access to resources which are ubiquitous and immediate. The issues facing the work-based learner no longer centre on the quest for information, but rather on how to evaluate that information which is available in the light of specifically identified purposes. As Murray (2012) notes:

> *"... with so much information now available and easy to share online, many universities are already reporting a decrease in footfall in their libraries ...".*

What need is there for the imposing classical porticos, the steel and glass towers of the academy with their daunting shadows when the information might be accessed within the comfort of the chair in one's home or workplace?

Given the seemingly inexhaustible proliferation of communications technologies and the impact of social media, the traditional educational institution could well find itself trying to establish an identity and purpose in a world changing at a pace with which those institutions are entirely unequipped to manage. As the need for impressive and expensive buildings disappears so too the role of teacher as gate-keeper of knowledge is brought into question, not least because access to information can be circumvented so simply. Undoubtedly a role exists as a mediator, a translator and knowledge broker, one who is able to guide, set contexts and facilitate the learner's engagement with the material, but the role of information dispenser and regulator becomes superfluous. Indeed there is already evidence (Maor, 2008) that students can make effective facilitators of learning and the emergence of an interdependency of classroom roles very similar to those outlined in the Learning in the Round approach. Maor's research which is concerned with online learning, suggests that there is still a role for the facilitator in terms of face-to-face interactions, providing that scaffolding that promotes insight and reflection as well as managing "... social or cognitive challenges ..." (Maor, 2008: 636). However what is clear is that facilitators will need to be far more flexible and responsive in order to be effective and that, as her title suggests, quite who is the teacher and who the learner, is a significant question.[3]

Learning in the Round and in the future

Envisaging future events can too easily lure one into apocalyptic visions of utopian and/or dystopian states. Previously we have witnessed predicted scenarios; Tofler's (1971) notion of 'Future shock,' Capra's (1982) 'Turning Point' and Stevenson's (2012) 'Optimist's tour of the future.' All are cases in point, all seemingly entirely plausible analyses of antecedents and credible

---

3   It is salutary to note the 2008 publication date of this article.

futures, and the evidence of their predictions is there to see, though without cataclysmic manifestations. It seems that the combined forces of governments, communications and social media, have precipitated some tipping point and that a climacteric could well be at hand. Policy-makers and politicians appear to be in retreat concerning support for education, beyond exhortation, vague murmurings of 'alternative provision' and evermore rigorous auditing regimes. Young people, be they students or not, are realising modes of living and communicating radically different, even alien to the worlds of their parents. Merged through communications platforms and social media with countless alternative and vicarious realities in which information is instantly accessible and awaits only conversion into meaningful knowledge, the province and possession of the privileged guardians is under threat.

Marina Gorbis' notion of socialstructed learning outlines a possible future context:

> *"We are moving away from the model in which learning is organized around stable, usually hierarchical institutions (schools, colleges, universities) that, for better and worse, have served as the main gateways to education and social mobility. Replacing that model is a new system in which learning is best conceived of as a flow, where learning resources are not scarce but widely available, opportunities for learning are abundant, and learners increasingly have the ability to autonomously dip into and out of continuous learning flows."*
> **(Gorbis, 2013)**

In the United Kingdom, Janet Murray in a compilation of opinions collected through a Guardian Blog, noted:

> *"With smartphones, tablets and other forms of technology at their disposal, today's students want a flexible approach to learning, where they can access resources or catch up on lectures at any time of the day or night... One contributor said that the traditional university campus could be "in the minority" as little as 10 years from now. Another predicted a "Yo! Sushi" style approach to higher education, where students pick up degree modules from different courses and institutions, combining face-to-face learning with online tutorials and lectures."*
> **(Murray, 2012)**

"Yo Sushi!" Now there's an idea with which to grapple.

The consequences of such a situation are clearly profound, not only for the individual learner, but for those involved in education. There is no doubt that technological progress has had the effect of shrinking the universe as access to knowledge (or at least, information) is rendered so much easier. At the same time for the individual mind this reality provides opportunities for exponential expansion, limited only by the extent to which the individual can use her/his imagination and exercise conscious discrimination in the selection of material with which to work. When this individual is readily able to engage with other like-minded and committed actors, then the consequences for developing self-motivated, autonomous and effective learners ironically may well be able to bring about some of the more hyperbolic goals currently featuring in educational policy. The possible implications for access and self-directed learning likely to be consequent upon the launch of GoogleGlass will be far-reaching, representing yet another step in learning availability and transformative capacities.

Throughout this book we have made much of the social nature of learning, of the importance of creating and working with a community of practitioners in which sharing, openness and collaboration in the quest for understanding and knowledge are central. Indeed the relationship between teacher and learner, it is claimed (Attwood, 2009) is a distinctive, perhaps even unique and intimate feature of UK tertiary education, which promotes learning and consolidates and extends that learning through the countless opportunities for feedback that it presents. Learning in the Round represents an approach to harnessing the individual and collective energies of its participants which might well prove to be effective as well as emancipatory.

Lest we drift too far into hyberbole ourselves and forget the realities with which work-based learning facilitators are concerned, it is helpful to conclude with a quotation from Reeders, whose caveats of a decade ago still ring true. Observing that 'classroom experience has a tendency to become too safe, bloodless and narcotic in its abstraction from life', Reeders goes on to emphasise how the forms of work-based learning vary and are markedly different to those of the academy:

> *"There are vague beliefs, complex policies, uncertain knowledge, short timelines, sketchy feedback, overlapping or unclear roles and oral presentation of results ... Like the Wild West the workplace is also often unpleasant or destructive and should not be romanticised."*
> *(Reeders, 2000: 210)*

Postscript

The origins of this book lay in the authors' interests in, and practice of, work-based learning and their desire to disseminate its ideas and concepts in order to make them available for the critical scrutiny of a wider audience. In so doing a range of interesting and challenging dilemmas has emerged with which we continue to grapple.

The first of these centres upon the notion that knowledge and learning reside within institutional structures and are the province of learned academics. What has emerged from our exposition is that the dismantling of these structures, and the consequent access to knowledge for a wider community, have attracted a more diverse audience of participants to learning. Secondly, traditional notions of learning and teaching are no longer viable in many areas, especially in the realm of work-based learning. Finally, issues such as accreditation, award structures and levels, and assessment regimes cease to exert and perpetuate hierarchical notions of achievement as approaches such as Learning in the Round gradually erode their rationales and question their efficacy.

Thus the question has to be asked, does Learning in the Round not only meet the criteria laid down by successive governments to expand the franchise of educational participation; but does it also provide answers to the perennial questions surrounding the access to and integration of commercial partners into tertiary education?

References

Attwood, R. (2009). The personal touch. Times Higher. 7th May.

Capra, F. (1982). The turning point: science, society and the rising culture. London. Fontana.

Dalrymple, R., Kemp. C., and Smith, P. (2012). Conceptualising work-based learning as a triadic learning endeavour. Journal of Further and Higher Education. iFirst, 1-15.

Dennen, V.P. (2005). From message posting to learning dialogues: factors affecting learner participation in asynchronous discussion. Distance Education 26:, 127-48.

Dennett, D. (2013). Seven rules for clearer, more effective thinking. The Observer. (The New Review). 19th May 2013. 20 – 21.

Eisner, E. (2000). Those who ignore the past...12 'easy' lessons for the new millennium. Journal of Curriculum Studies. 32 (2). 343 – 357.

Felce, A. (2010). Towards a Context-engaged Approach to Work-Based Learning. Learning and Teaching in Higher Education 4:1, 20-35.

Gibbons, M. Limoges, C. Nowotny, H. Schwartzman, S. Scott, P. & Trow, M. (1994). The new production of knowledge: the dynamics of science and research in contemporary societies. London. Sage.

Gorbis, M. (2013). The nature of the future: dispatches from the socialstructed world. New York. Free Press. http://www.fastcoexist.com/1681507/ Accessed 16th August 2013.

Hodge, P., Wright, S., Barraket, J., Scott, M., Melville, R., and Richardson, S. (2011) Revisiting 'how we learn' in academia: practice-based learning exchanges in three Australian universities, Studies in Higher Education, 36(2), 167 - 183.

Jones, C. & Shao, B. (2011). The net generation and digital natives: implications for higher education. York. Higher Educational Academy.

Maor, D. (2008). Changing relationship: who is the learner and who is the teacher in the online educational landscape?" Australasian Journal of Educational Technology. 24 (1). 627 – 638.

Moore, T. & Workman, B. (2011) Work-Based Learning: Creative, Imaginative and Flexible Approaches. International Journal of Learning 17. (12). 67 - 80.

Murray, J. (2012). http://www.theguardian.com/higher-education-network/higher-education-network-blog 17th April.

Niea, M., Alejandro A., Witthausa, G. & Barklambb, K. (2011). How do e-book readers enhance learning opportunities for distance work-based learners? Research in Learning Technology 19 (1). 19 - 38.

Open University (2006). Work-Based Learning: Models and Approaches Buckingham: Open University.

Reeders, E. (2000). Scholarly practice in work-based learning: fitting the glass slipper. Higher Education Research & Development. 19 (2). 205 – 220.

Reeve, F. and Gallacher, J. (2005) 'Employer-based "partnerships": a key problem for work-based learning programmes?', Journal of Education and Work 18:2, 219-33.

Scott, I. (2010) 'But I know that already.' Rhetoric or reality? The accreditation of prior experiential learning in the context of work-based learning', International Journal of Lifelong Education, 19 – 31.

Stevenson, M. (2012). An optimist's tour of the future. London. Profile Books.

Tofler, A. (1970). Future shock. New York. Random House.

Tuan, Y. (1974). Topophilia, a study of environmental perception, attitude and values. New Jersey. Prentice Hall.

Index